# Flowers from the Desert

# FLOWERS FROM THE DESERT

Sayings on Humility, Obedience,
Repentance, and Love from
the Christian Hermits
of Ancient Times

Translated from the Greek,
compiled, and arranged by

Archbishop Chrysostomos of Etna

Etna, California
2003

Originally published in Romanian: Arhiepiscopul Chrysostomos al Etnei, *Flori din Deșert: Pilde Despre Smerenie, Ascultare, Pocăință și Iubire ale Sihaștrilor Creștini din Vechime,* traduse din engleză de Remus Rus (București: Editura Vremea XXI, 2003)

(ISBN 937–645–043–0)

LIBRARY OF CONGRESS CONTROL NUMBER

2003110211

ISBN 0–911165–54–1

# THE AUTHOR

*The Most Reverend Chrysostomos* received his undergraduate and graduate education in general and Byzantine history at the University of California, his undergraduate and graduate education in psychology at the California State University and at Princeton University, where he received his doctoral degree, and the Licentiate in Orthodox Theological Studies from the Center for Traditionalist Orthodox Studies in Etna, California, where he is currently a Senior Scholar. He has held professorial posts at the University of California, Ashland Theological Seminary, and Ashland University. He has also been a visiting professor at the Institute of Theology at Uppsala University, in Sweden, and, as a Senior Fulbright Scholar in Romania, at the University of Bucharest, the Alexandru I. Cuza University, and the Ion Mincu University of Architecture and Urbanism, where he is an adjunct professor. His Eminence was a visiting scholar at the Harvard Divinity School in 1983 and, in 1985, at Oxford University, under the sponsorship of the Marsden Foundation. He is a also a former summer fellow of the National Endowment for the Humanities and, more recently, former Executive Director of the United States Fulbright Commission in Romania.

ENGLISH TRANSLATIONS FROM THE DESERT FATHERS
BY ARCHBISHOP CHRYSOSTOMOS

*The Ancient Fathers of the Desert*
(Hellenic College Press, 1980)

*The Ancient Fathers of the Desert: A Second Volume*
(Hellenic College Press, 1986)

*The Evergetinos: A Complete Text*
eight volumes to date
(Center for Traditionalist Orthodox Studies, 1988–)

## Acknowledgements

I am very much indebted to the Fulbright Commission in Romania, and especially Dr. Oana Popa, Ioana Ieronim, and Manuela Brusalis, for encouraging me, during my time as a Fulbright Scholar in that country, to write and publish this compendium. It is my hope that this and other studies and publications that have risen out of my Fulbright appointment will help to strengthen the Fulbright program, America's flagship exchange program for scholars and professors, and serve as a token of my appreciation for the opportunities and memorable scholarly and personal benefits which it afforded me during the academic year that I lectured and taught in Romania.

I should note that when I later returned to Bucharest, from 2002 to 2003, as Exective Director of the u. s. Fulbright Commission in Romania, I further benefited from the kindness and friendship of Mrs. Ieronim (now retired from her post at the Commission) and Mrs. Brusalis, as well as from the support and advice of Dr. Popa, who is now an advisor to the Romanian President and Chief of the North American Desk at the Ministry of Foreign Affairs.

I would also like to express my appreciation to the faculties of history and economics at the University of Bucharest and the Alexandru I. Cuza University in Iași, as well as the teaching staff at the Ion Mincu University of Architecture and Urbanism in Bucharest, for providing me with both the time and facilities, amidst my Fulbright teaching duties, to pursue my translating and writing. At the Ion Mincu University, with which I still maintain an adjunct academic affiliation, I met Dr. Augustin Ioan, the gifted Romanian architect, poet, and scholar. To him I owe a special debt of gratitude for team teaching with me during my Fulbright assignment and, in our subsequent collaboration, for his dauntless support of my work and for the personal kindness that he and his charming wife, Dr. Simona Ioan, have shown me.

Finally, I would like to thank Mrs. Silvia Colfescu, Director of Editura Vremea, the Bucharest publishing house, who has, to date, published four of the six books of mine that have appeared in Romania, including the Romanian edition of this volume, which was launched at the Bucharest Book Fair in the spring of 2003.

# CONTENTS

# INTRODUCTION

For nearly thirty years now, after becoming a monk rather late in life and after having lived a normal "life in the world," as the Desert Fathers might have expressed it, I have been reading and translating from Greek the writings of these practitioners—who lived and flourished in the first few centuries of the Christian era—of a philosophical and spiritual life that remains to this day a blossom in the wilderness of the demons of human deceit and vanity. In the early 1980s, when I was a Visiting Scholar to the Harvard Divinity School, I began a series of books on the psychology of the Desert Fathers, drawing from their aphorisms and from stories of their monastic struggles a profile of the elements by which, in the language of the Eastern Orthodox spiritual tradition, one ascends the ladder of Divine ascent, purifying the emotions and passions and becoming one with the Energies of God: perfected within the imperfection of this world. In the mid- and late-1980s, at Oxford University in England, under the sponsorship of the Marsden Foundation, and then while teaching as a Visiting Professor at the Theological Institute of Uppsala University in Sweden, I subsequently wrote four small volumes on these elements: humility, obedience, repentance, and love.

The unifying theme of these books is that the struggle for human perfection within the imperfections of the world and the human psyche begins, according to the teachings of the Desert Fathers, by a humble acknowledgement of the depths of human depravity *face à face* with the human potential for divinization (in Greek, θέωσις, or union with the energies—though not the essence—of God) and perfection. Having beheld the higher spiritual ideals and principles of human life, a spiritual aspirant must then develop a profound commitment to such things. In this commitment, he learns to obey and to submit to the good, to the Divine, as well as to those things and persons that represent, and guide one towards, the higher life: consciously following in obedience and with fidelity the quiet invitation of the heart to partake

of the good things (τὰ ἀγαθά, in Greek) of the inner life of the
soul. Seeing, at last, how far short he falls of the standard of perfection, an aspirant is overcome, not by self-denigrating guilt, but
by a deep, ineluctable regret before all that separates the human
from the holy. In keeping with the true meaning of the Greek
word for repentance, μετάνοια, the aspirant undergoes a complete
realignment of the thoughts, turning the mind naturally and
spontaneously to the good. Sorrow for sin, strangely joined to an
ineffable joy, creates a condition in which—pierced to the heart
by contrition and seemingly overwhelmed by a sense of unwor-
thiness and an intense fear of certain perdition—the repentant
struggler draws nearer to God in his burning awareness of what it
is that separates him from what is so close. The gap between God
and the sinner, in this repentant state, is closed, not by self-affir-
mations about salvation and holiness, but by a sure Grace that
operates within joyous sorrow.

Finally, having ascended through lowliness to the loftiness of
obedience, and having cultivated the desire for God which repentance brings, the spiritual seeker is drawn to God by love, reaching the highest rung on the spiritual ladder that leads up to virtue and perfection. Not by compulsion, but by the energy and
action of God, he is united to the Divine, transformed thereby in
love. Subject to sin but drawn by love to perfection, *amor gignit
amorem*: love engenders love. So great is this love of God, that the
aspirant comes to see Him in his fellow man, making the whole
of life one of concern for others. He places even before self-dis-
cipline the sacred duty of loving service to one's neighbor; for, as
one holy man succinctly says, the love of one's brother is evidence
of one's love for God—the former verifies the latter. With a self-
effacing and humble love, one who is joined to God exalts the
very existence of others above his own, concealing his own virtues
and spiritual feats, lest he appear to be more than those whom he
is called to serve. He comes to that mastership which is true servitude, in the imitation of God's inimitable love. In the offering and
gracious acceptance of gentle hospitality, in the giving of alms, in

the forbearance of the shortcomings of others, and in the practical, tangible display of sincere care and affection for all, this servitude is made manifest and comes to fruition.

In conceiving the idea of a psychology of human transformation, a Patristic psychology drawn from the practical experience of the Desert Fathers, I had occasion to collect virtual volumes of aphorisms and anecdotes from these monks and nuns of the wilderness (and, indeed, the term "Fathers" is an inclusive one; the desert *Abba*, or Father, has his counterpart in the desert *Amma*, or Mother). I have become involved, as a direct result of this, in a project which has been slowly producing, since 1988, the first full text in English of the standard Greek collection of the sayings of the Desert Fathers, the *Evergetinos*, which in the Greek is contained in four books. To date, eight English volumes have been published from the first two books of the Greek text. It is from my earlier research on the psychology of the Fathers and this present translation work that I have drawn and selected the sayings contained in this book. Many of them, since almost all of the extant translations of aphorisms and anecdotes from the desert hermits are from Latin sources, appear here for the first time in their original form; indeed, some of the specific aphorisms of the Elders (originally collected in what was called the *Gerontikon*, from the Greek word γέρων, or Elder) are absent from the Latin collection. This Latin collection of aphorisms from the Desert Fathers dates to the sixth century and was likely first compiled by the Latin Deacon Pelagius, later Pope of Rome. It draws from various strata of earlier Greek manuscripts, probably written in the latter half of the fourth century and no doubt partly based on Coptic texts or oral traditions. These Greek manuscripts, many of which have not survived, were gathered into one single text in the eleventh century by the Byzantine Monk Paul, founder of the Mone Hyperagias Theotokou Evergetidos (the Monastery of the Mother of God the Benefactress); hence, the appellation given to this collection: the *Evergetinos*. It is the anthology which traditionally constituted the primary source of sayings from the Desert Fathers for the Orthodox Christian world.

In the eighteenth century, the *Evergetinos* was revised, edited, and published by Saint Nikodemos of the Holy Mountain, who, along with Saint Makarios of Corinth, was also responsible for the compilation of the monumental *Philokalia*, a collection of spiritual texts drawn from the Byzantine mystics. Saint Nikodemos' text of the *Evergetinos*, which is arranged around certain "hypotheses" or "themes" concerning the monastic estate and spiritual life in general, is written in a style of Greek that is often cryptic, laconic, and rich with irony. In many instances, the aphorisms of the Fathers and the anecdotes which they tell are in the form of a classical riddle or a play on words or thoughts. The manner in which they are written, therefore, demands concentration and a moment of reflection, to be properly understood. These traits tremendously enhance the impact of the sayings of the Desert Fathers in Greek. However, because this enhancement is accomplished by the use of rhetorical traditions and devices that are common to antiquity but rare in modern languages, the sayings at times lose much in translation. This is to some extent also true in modern Greek, though to a much lesser degree than in other languages. The several translations of the original Greek of the *Evergetinos* into modern Greek have, in fact, helped to flesh out the skeletal form of the original, while still retaining many of the idioms and linguistic peculiarities of the older Greek. These texts, available to the general reader with a reasonable proficiency in modern Greek, though not perfect, surpass, in my mind, anything to be found in translations from Latin sources into modern languages.

Therefore, I have worked here, as in my other translations of texts from the Desert Fathers, with both the original Greek edition of the *Evergetinos* edited by Saint Nikodemos in the eighteenth century and with modern Greek renditions of his edition. At times, I have chosen to retain the terse expressions of the original Greek; at other times, without violating the style or content of the ancient text, I have directly translated from the modern Greek. The result is, I think, the closest possible approximation of the tone, spirit, and meaning of the original texts that can be found in a contemporary language, other than modern Greek, and one which easily and adequately translates into other modern languages. Hence, I believe that my translation offers a genuine encounter with the wisdom of the Desert Fathers that eludes translations made from the Latin source texts.

As a final note, the reader will see that I have not used the Latin forms of names and place-names, but have left them in their original Greek form. This is important, not only because one retains, with such a device, certain qualities of the original text, but because some of the names in Greek are renderings of Coptic and Syriac names that have otherwise been lost in the historical past. It is probably better to retain these names as they exist in the extant manuscript tradition, thus bearing testimony—if imperfectly and by derivation—to the origins of many of the spiritual traditions which have formed Greek and other Orthodox spiritual traditions and that have, of course, impacted on the spiritual development of Western Christianity, too.

*Archbishop Chrysostomos*
*Bucharest, Romania*
*January, 2001*

# CHAPTER I

## *HUMILITY*

An Elder said, "I prefer a defeat accompanied by humility to a victory accompanied by pride."

\* \* \*

Abba Sarmatias said, "I prefer a sinful man who nonetheless recognizes that he has sinned, and who repents, to a man who has not sinned and fancies that he is perhaps virtuous."

\* \* \*

An Elder said, "Humility has often saved many, even without effort; this is demonstrated by the Publican and the Prodigal Son, who said only a few words and were saved."

\* \* \*

Abba Epiphanios used to say that the Canaanite woman wept and was heeded; the woman with an issue of blood approached in silence and was praised; the Publican did not open his mouth at all, and yet his prayer was heard by God; while the Pharisee shouted and was condemned.

\* \* \*

Abba Isaiah said, "We need humility more than any other virtue; let us always be ready, whatever word we might say or hear, or whatever we might do, to say, 'Forgive me'; for through humility, all of the evil works of the Devil are foiled."

\* \* \*

An Elder said, "He who has humility humbles the demons; he who does not have humility is a plaything of the demons."

\* \* \*

Abba Hyperechios said, "Humility is a tree of life that rises up to the height of Heaven."

❋　❋　❋

The Elders used to say, "Humility is a crown for the monk."

❋　❋　❋

An Elder was once asked when the soul acquires humility. He answered, "When it thinks about its own vices."

❋　❋　❋

An Elder said, "Just as the earth never falls down, neither does the man who humbles himself."

❋　❋　❋

An Elder was asked, "What is humility?"

He replied, "When your brother sins against you and you forgive him before he asks your forgiveness."

❋　❋　❋

A brother asked an Elder, "What does it mean for a man to progress in Godliness?"

"A man's progress is in his humility," replied the Elder. "The more a man descends to humility, the more he is raised up in progress."

❋　❋　❋

The Elders used to say that when we are not undergoing warfare, it is then that we are in greater need of being humbled, since God, knowing our infirmity, covers us. But if we are boastful, God removes His protection from us and we slip into perdition.

❋　❋　❋

One of the Fathers related that there was an diligent Elder in the *Kellia* [isolated monastic cells], who wore a garment made of woven rushes. On one occasion, he visited Abba Ammonas.

When Abba Ammonas saw him wearing the straw garment, he said, "This does you no good at all."

The Elder then asked Abba Ammonas, "Father, there are three thoughts that bother me: specifically, whether I should go into the desert regions, or depart to a foreign place, where nobody knows me, or shut myself up in my cell and have no dealings with anyone, eating every second day. Which of these should I choose?"

Abba Ammonas answered, "It will not benefit you to carry out any of these three thoughts; it is preferable, if you wish to hear me, to stay in your cell and eat a small amount each day, always keeping the words of the Publican in your heart; then you can be saved."

✼   ✼   ✼

A brother went to the mountain of Pherme to visit a great Elder, and said to him, "Abba, what am I to do, for my soul is perishing?"

"Why so, my child?" asked the Elder.

"When I was in the world," replied the brother, "I fasted gladly, kept vigil a great deal, and felt much compunction and fervent zeal; but now I do not see anything good in my soul."

The Elder responded to him, "Believe me, child, whatever you did when you were in the world was not acceptable to God, because in doing these things you were urged on by vainglory and the praise of men. This is why Satan did not make war on you. He had no interest in breaking your eagerness, because you derived no benefit from it whatever.

"But now, when he sees that you have been called by Christ and are His soldier, and have come forth to oppose him, he has armed himself against you. Thus, the one Psalm that you say now with compunction is more pleasing to God than the thousands that you used to say in the world. Here, God more readily accepts your small amount of fasting than the weeks of fasting that you undertook in the world."

"Now I do not fast at all," answered the brother; "rather, I have lost all the good things that I had in the world."

"What you have now is sufficient for you," said the Elder; "only be patient and it will be well with you."

But the brother persisted and said, "Abba, my soul is perishing."

The Elder then replied to him, "Believe me, brother, I did not want to say this to you, so as not to destroy your solicitude; but since I see that Satan has brought you to a state of despair, I tell you: It is prideful for you to suppose that when you were in the world you did good and lived well; for this is how the Pharisee thought (when he was boasting in the Temple), and he lost all the good that he had accomplished. Now if, on the other hand, you think that you are not doing anything good, this is sufficient for you to be saved; for this is humility. It was in this way (through humility and self-deprecation) that the Publican, who had done nothing good, was justified. A sinful and negligent man who feels contrition of heart and humility is more pleasing before God than one who does many good deeds, but is of the opinion that he has completely succeeded in accomplishing something good."

Receiving great benefit from this reply of the Abba, the brother made a prostration to the Elder and said to him: "Today, Abba, my soul has been saved because of you."

❖    ❖    ❖

In a certain city there lived a Bishop who, by the activity of Satan, fell into fornication. A few days later there was a Liturgy in the Church, and, without anyone having known of the Bishop's sin, he nonetheless made his confession in front of all the people, saying, "I have fallen into fornication." As soon as he had uttered these words, he took off his *Omophorion* [Bishop's stole] and placed it on the Holy Table. "I can no longer be a Bishop," he said.

In the wake of this scene of sincere confession, the people were all seized with emotion and cried out in lamentation, "Let this sin be upon us; only remain in the Episcopate."

"If you want me to remain with you," answered the Bishop, "do what I tell you." He immediately ordered that all of the doors of the Church be shut, fell on his face at a side door, and said to the people, "Anyone who does not tread on me when he leaves the Church is not on the side of God."

All of the people did as the Bishop told them; that is to say, they trod on him as they departed. As the last person left, a voice was heard from Heaven saying, "I have forgiven the Bishop of his sin because of his great humility."

✳   ✳   ✳

Abba Anthony said, "I saw all the snares of the Devil spread out over all the earth, and I groaned and said, 'What is it that bypasses these, without being trapped?' And I heard a voice saying to me, 'Humility.'"

✳   ✳   ✳

The same Elder said to Abba Poimen, "A man's work is this: to assume responsibility for his sin before God and to expect temptation until his last breath."

✳   ✳   ✳

Demons once rose up against Abba Arsenios and harassed him in his cell. When those who served him came and stood outside his cell, they heard him crying to God and saying, "O my God, do not abandon me, for I have never done anything good in Thy sight. But grant me according to the measure of Thy goodness to make a beginning."

✳   ✳   ✳

A brother visited Abba Ammonas and said to him, "Abba, give me a word." He stayed with the Elder for seven days, but heard nothing from him.

Then, when he was leaving, Abba Ammonas said to him, as he escorted him out, "Even to this day, my sins are a wall of darkness between me and God."

✻   ✻   ✻

Abba Daniel recounted that there once lived in Babylon a young woman, the daughter of a governor of that place, who had a demon inside her. The father of this girl knew a monk, whom he loved and whom he persisted in asking to heal his daughter. The monk replied to him, "No one can heal your daughter, except some anchorites whom I know. But if we summon them, out of modesty they will not consent to do such a thing. It is preferable for us to do the following: When they come to market to sell their handiwork, pretend that you want to buy their wares, and invite them to your house in order to give them the money. When they come, ask them to pray for your daughter; I believe that if they do this, she will be cured."

So, they went out to the marketplace and found the disciple of a certain Elder, who was sitting there to sell his handiwork. The governor's men took him and his baskets and led him to the governor's residence, so that he might receive payment for his wares. Now, as soon as he entered, the demonized girl ran up to him and slapped him. The monk then turned the other cheek, putting into practice the commandment of the Lord: "Whosoever shall smite thee on thy right cheek, turn to him the other also" [St. Matthew 5:39]. This behavior tormented the demon, who said with ghastly cries, "O such violence! The commandment of Jesus expels me," and immediately left the woman; at that moment, she became healthy and returned to her right mind. This incident was made known to the Elders, who glorified God and said that nothing so annihilates the pride of the Devil as the humility that the commandments of Christ inspire.

✻   ✻   ✻

Abba Carion said: "I have toiled more than my son Zacharias, and yet I have not attained to the measure of his virtue, on account of his humility and silence."

❀    ❀    ❀

On one occasion, when the same Abba Zacharias was staying in Sketis [a monastic community in the Egyptian desert], he had a vision. He arose at once and reported it to his Elder, Abba Carion. The latter, being a practical man, had no knowledge of these phenomena. He got up from where he was sitting and thrashed Zacharias, saying, "Perhaps this vision came from demons." But since Abba Zacharias continued to have the vision, he left his cell one night and went to Abba Poimen.

After finding Abba Poimen, he recounted the vision to him and how he felt a burning sensation inside himself. The Elder realized that this phenomenon came from God and said to Zacharias: "Go to such-and-such an Elder and take to heart whatever he tells you."

Abba Zacharias went off to this Elder, who, before Zacharias even opened his mouth and told him anything, gave a detailed account of his situation and said to him in conclusion, "This vision is from God, but go and submit to your spiritual Father."

❀    ❀    ❀

Abba Moses once asked this same Zacharias, "Tell me, Elder, what should I do?"

No sooner did Abba Zacharias hear this, than he fell at the Abba's feet and said to him, "Are you asking me, Father?"

Abba Moses then said to him, "Believe me, Zacharias, my child, I saw the Holy Spirit descending on you and that is why I am compelled to ask you."

Zacharias then took his *koukoulion* [monastic headcovering] from his head and placed it under his feet; and trampling on it, he said, "Unless a man is crushed in this way, he cannot be a monk."

❋   ❋   ❋

Abba Poimen related that when Abba Zacharias was about to die, Abba Moses asked him, "What do you see, Abba?"

He replied, "Is it not better to be silent, Father?"

"Yes, my child," responded Abba Moses, "be silent."

At the moment of his death, Abba Isidore, who was sitting nearby, raised his eyes to Heaven and said, "Rejoice, Zacharias, my child, because the gates of the Kingdom of Heaven have been opened for you."

❋   ❋   ❋

The esteemed Archbishop Theophilos once went to the mountain of Nitria. He was visited by the spiritual Father of the ascetics of that mountain. The Archbishop asked him, "Father, what further have you discovered on this path of asceticism?"

The Elder answered, "Always to consider ourselves blame-worthy for everything and to reproach ourselves."

"Truly," the Archbishop agreed, "there is no other way than this."

❋   ❋   ❋

When the same Archbishop went to Sketis, the brothers gathered together and said to Abba Pambo, "Say a word to the Pope [the ancient title given to the Bishop of Alexandria], that he might be edified."

The Elder replied, "If he does not profit from my silence, nei-ther will he profit from my speech."

❋   ❋   ❋

Abba Evagrios said, "The beginning of salvation is for a man to reproach himself."

❋   ❋   ❋

Abba Theodore was once relaxing with some other monks. While they were eating, they took up their glasses in silence and did not say the familiar invocation, "Forgive me."

Abba Theodore then said, "Monks have lost their manners by not saying, 'Forgive me.'"

❀    ❀    ❀

A brother once told the same Abba Theodore, "I want to fulfill the commandments."

The Elder replied to him, "Abba Thomas once said, 'I want to fulfill my thoughts as God wills.' So he immediately went to the oven and made bread. When asked by some paupers, he gave them all of the bread. When some other paupers asked him for alms, he gave them the baskets in which he kept the bread, as well as the garment that he was wearing. He went into his cell wearing only the *maphorion* [a monastic shawl] which monks throw around their shoulders; but even after such almsgiving, he reproached himself, saying: 'I have not fulfilled the commandment of God as I should have done.'"

❀    ❀    ❀

A brother said to Abba Theodore, "Give me a word of consolation, for I am perishing."

And then, with sorrow, Abba Theodore replied, "I am in danger of perishing, and thus what can I tell you?"

❊    ❊    ❊

Amma Theodora used to say that neither asceticism nor hardship, nor any kind of toil, saves, except for genuine humility. She told this story: "There was an anchorite who was going to exorcise some demons. First, he asked them, 'By what power are you driven from a man? By fasting?'

"'We neither eat nor drink,' they replied.

"'By vigil?'

"And they said, 'We do not sleep at all.'

"'By withdrawal from the world?'

"'No,' they answered, 'we inhabit the deserts.'

"When the Elder persisted in asking in what way they were driven out, they confessed, 'Nothing defeats us except humility.'"

❀ ❀ ❀

Abba John the Short said, "Humility and fear of God are above all the other virtues."

❀ ❀ ❀

Again, he said, "Who sold Joseph?"

One of the brothers responded, "His brothers."

"No," the Elder rejoined, "it was his humility that sold him. He could have said, when he was being sold, 'I am your brother,' and argued with them. But in silence and humility he let himself be sold; and his humility made him the ruler of Egypt.'"

❀ ❀ ❀

Again, he said, "Having let go of a light burden, namely self-reproach, we have taken up the heaviest; namely, self-justification."

❀ ❀ ❀

One of the Fathers said about Abba John that "through his humility, he has the whole of Sketis hanging on his little finger."

❀ ❀ ❀

Abba John the Theban said, "A monk should attain humility before all else; for this is the first commandment of the Savior, Who said, 'Blessed are the poor in spirit: for theirs is the Kingdom of Heaven'" [St. Matthew 5:3].

❀ ❀ ❀

Abba Matoes said, "The closer a man comes to God, all the more does he see himself to be a sinner; for when the Prophet Isaiah saw God in his vision, he called himself wretched and unclean."

❄    ❄    ❄

The same Elder said, "When I was young, I thought that I was perhaps doing something good; but now that I am an old man, I see that I have not even one good deed to show."

A brother asked Abba Matoes, "How is it that the monks of Sketis succeed in doing more than the commandment says, that is, in loving their enemies more than themselves?"

"Up to now," replied the Elder, "I have not loved even Him Who loves me as much as I love myself."

❋    ❋    ❋

Abba Jacob said, "I once visited Abba Matoes, and as I was leaving I said to him, 'I want to visit the hermits' cells.'

"'Greet Abba John on my behalf,' said the Elder.

"So when I went to Abba John, I told him, 'Abba Matoes greets you.'

"The Elder responded with delight, 'Abba Matoes is "an Israelite indeed, in whom is no guile!"'" [St. John 1:47].

"After a year I visited Abba Matoes again, and conveyed Abba John's greeting to him. He answered modestly, 'I am not worthy of the Elder's praise. Know this, however: that when you hear an Elder honoring his neighbor more than himself, you can be sure that this man has attained to great heights; for this is precisely what perfection is, that a man honors his neighbor more than himself.'"

❄    ❄    ❄

A brother besought Abba Matoes, "Father, say something that will benefit me."

"Go and beseech God," replied the Elder, "to give you mourning and humility in your heart; always be mindful of your sins; never judge others, but become lower than everyone else. Cut off familiarity from yourself and restrain your tongue and your belly; and if someone talks about a certain subject, do not argue with him; but if he speaks well, say 'Yes' to him, and if he speaks badly, tell him, 'You know what you are talking about,' and do not quarrel with him about what he has said. This is humility."

\*   \*   \*

A brother asked Abba Alonios, "What does it mean to debase oneself?"

The Elder answered, "It means to believe that you are lower even than the dumb beasts and to recognize that they, unlike you, are not accountable for what they do."

\*   \*   \*

Abba Xanthias said, "A dog is better than I, for he has love and does not judge."

\*   \*   \*

Abba Poimen said about Abba Isidore that every night he would braid a bundle of palm branches; and the brothers, seeing him toil, would beseech him, saying, "Relax a little, for you are now old."

But he would reply to them, "Even if they burn Isidore and scatter his ashes to the wind, I will still have no respite; for the Son of God came into the world for our sake."

\*   \*   \*

The same Elder said likewise about Abba Isidore, that when his thoughts said to him, "You are now a great ascetic," he would reply to them, "Am I perhaps like Abba Anthony? Or perhaps I have become perfect like Abba Pambo? Or, finally, perhaps I have attained the stature of the other Fathers who pleased God?" By responding in this way he gave himself rest, and the thoughts would withdraw and flee. When, once more, the enemies of our soul, the demons, caused him to be discouraged, by telling him that after all this he would be cast into Hell, he replied to them, "Even if I am cast into Hell, I will assuredly find you beneath me."

❋   ❋   ❋

Abba Poimen said that when a man reproaches himself, he will have endurance and patience in every circumstance.

❋   ❋   ❋

The same Elder said that when a man succeeds in grasping the saying of the Apostle, "Unto the pure all things are pure" [St. Titus 1:15], he sees himself as being lower than all of God's creatures. A brother who heard this said to him, "How can I reckon myself lower than a murderer?"

The Elder replied, "If a man attains to the measure of this saying, such that he acquires purity, and sees a man engaging in murder, he will say, 'He has committed only this one sin; but I commit murder daily.'"

❋   ❋   ❋

The same brother put the same question also to Abba Anoub, telling him the opinion of Abba Poimen. On hearing him, Abba Anoub replied, "What he told you was right; this is how it is. For if a man attains to the measure of this saying, such that he acquires purity and sees the sins of his brother, he succeeds, by the power of his virtue, in swallowing them up (that is, in overlooking them)."

"And what is this virtue?" asked the brother a second time.

"Self-reproach," answered Abba Anoub; "for he who reproaches himself justifies his neighbor, and this righteousness conceals his neighbor's sins."

❋   ❋   ❋

It was said of Abba Poimen that he was never willing to maintain his own opinion against that of another Elder (or even to give the appearance of so doing); thus, he would praise him, regardless of the situation. Indeed, those who knew him related the following: If he was visited by some believers, he would first send them to Abba Anoub, since the latter was his senior in years. For his part, Abba Anoub would tell them, "Go to my brother Poimen, because he has the gift of teaching." If at any time it happened that Abba Anoub and Abba Poimen were sitting together, Abba Poimen did not speak at all, since Abba Anoub was present.

❋  ❋  ❋

Abba Poimen used to tell how he heard the blessed Abba Anthony say, "The greatest deed that a man can do is to assume responsibility for his sin before God and expect temptation until his last breath."

❋  ❋  ❋

On another occasion, Abba Poimen said, groaning, "All of the virtues have entered this house, except for one; without it a man suffers torment and vexation."

"Which is this?" he was asked.

He replied, "That a man should reproach himself."

❋  ❋  ❋

Abba Poimen said, "I say that wherever Satan is hurled, there I, too, am hurled."

❋  ❋  ❋

Again, he said, "A man always needs humility and the fear of God, just as he needs air in order to breathe."

❋  ❋  ❋

The same Abba said, "Humbling yourself before God, reckoning that you are nothing, and setting aside your will—all of these are tools of the soul."

❋  ❋  ❋

On another occasion he said, "The Elders were once sitting at the table, and Abba Alonios was standing up and serving them as they ate. The Elders praised him, but he did not reply at all. One of the Elders then said to him privately, 'Why did you not respond at all to the Elders when they praised you?'

"'If I were to respond to them,' said Abba Alonios, 'I would be accepting their praise.'"

❄   ❄   ❄

A brother asked Abba Poimen, "To what should I attend, when I am sitting in my cell?"

"To this day," replied the Elder, "I am a man who has been submerged in mud up to his neck, carrying a heavy burden around my neck and crying out to God, 'Have mercy on me.'"

❄   ❄   ❄

The same Elder said, "If a brother visits you and you see that you are deriving no benefit at all from his coming, look into your mind and find out what thought you had before the brother came to your cell. From this examination you will understand what it was that made this visit unprofitable and that you were the cause of it. If you carry out this advice with humility, you will be blameless with regard to your neighbor, since you will blame yourself and will bear the burden of your own faults. If a man sits piously in his cell, he will not sin; for God is ever before him. As I see it, a man acquires fear of God by remaining piously in his cell."

❄   ❄   ❄

Abba Sisoes said, "He who knowingly possesses humility fulfills the whole of Scripture."

❄   ❄   ❄

A brother once visited Abba Sisoes on the mountain of Abba Anthony; while they were conversing, he asked the Elder, "Father, have you not by now attained to the stature of Abba Anthony?"

"If I had a single one of Abba Anthony's thoughts," answered Abba Sisoes, "I would be ablaze."

Another brother asked him, "Abba, I perceive that the remembrance of God remains with me."

"It is not important that your mind is with God," replied the Elder. "What is important is that you see yourself as being below all other creatures. This is why physical labor leads to humility."

❀   ❀   ❀

Abba Sisoes said to a brother, "How are you doing?"

"I waste my days, Father," answered the brother.

"If I were to waste a single day," said the Elder, "I would be grateful; that is to say, if I were to pass a single day without adding to my sins, I would be grateful."

❀   ❀   ❀

Three Elders once visited Abba Sisoes, after having heard of him. The first of them said to him, "Father, how can I be saved from the gnashing of teeth and the unsleeping worm?"

Abba Sisoes did not give him an answer.

The second asked, "Father, how can I be saved from the gnashing of teeth and the unsleeping worm?"

Abba Sisoes did not reply to him, either.

The third one said, "Father, what am I to do, for from my fear of the recollection of the outer darkness, I cannot even breathe?"

The Elder then said to them, "I do not think about any of these things, but I hope that God, compassionate as He is, will have mercy on me."

On hearing this reply, the Elders were upset and got up to leave. But Abba Sisoes, since he did not want to let them go away in distress, said to them, "You are blessed, brothers. Truly, I envy you, for if your minds are always dominated by such thoughts, it is impossible for you to sin. But what am I to do, hard-hearted as I am, for I have not been granted to know even whether there is a punishment for men? Because of this I sin every hour."

When the Elders heard these words of Abba Sisoes, they repented of their previous thoughts and said, "Just as we have heard, so too have we seen."

\*   \*   \*

Abba Sisoes used to say that the way that leads to humility is abstinence, unceasing prayer to God, and the struggle to be lower than every man.

\*   \*   \*

He also said that Scripture says about idols, "'They have a mouth, but shall not speak; eyes have they, and shall not see; ears have they, and shall not hear' [Psalm 113:5–6]. This is how a monk should also be; just as idols are an abomination, so also should he think that he is an abomination."

\*   \*   \*

A monk asked Abba Cronios, "Father, in what way does a man arrive at humility?"

"Through fear of God," replied the Elder.

"And how does he arrive at the fear of God?" the brother asked a second time.

"In my opinion," answered the Elder again, "it is by withdrawing oneself from everything, giving himself over to physical labor, and, as far as he is able, thinking about the departure of the soul from the body and the judgment of God."

\*   \*   \*

To a great anchorite who said, "Why do you make war on me, Satan?" Satan replied, "It is you, with your humility, who war mightily against me."

\*   \*   \*

On one occasion, Abba Macarios was returning from the marsh to his cell and was carrying palm leaves. The Devil met him on the road with a scythe. He tried to strike him, but was unable to do so; and then he said to him, "Great spiritual power emanates from you, Macarios, and this is why I cannot do anything against you; for see, whatever you do, that I do also: you fast, and so do I; you do not sleep, and I never sleep at all; there is only one respect in which you beat me."

"What is this?" Abba Macarios asked him.

"Your humility," the Devil answered, "and this is why I cannot do anything against you."

\* \* \*

An Elder was asked, "Why do demons war on us so much?"

"Because we throw our weapons away," answered the Elder; "and by weapons I mean dishonor, humility, non-acquisitiveness, and patience."

\* \* \*

The same Elder said, "Do not be humble only in speech, but also be humble of mind; for without humility it is impossible to be exalted in Godly works."

\* \* \*

Once upon a time there were two brothers in the flesh who lived in the same place; the Devil attempted to separate the one from the other. One day, when the younger was lighting a lamp, a demon set to work and turned over the lampstand, which knocked the lamp down. So, the older brother beat him in anger.

Instead of getting angry, the younger brother made a prostration and said to him, "Forgive me, my brother, and I will light it again."

With such humility from the younger brother, the power of the Lord immediately came forth and destroyed all of the demon's power; he went to his chief, who was residing in a pagan temple, and reported the event to him.

A pagan priest heard the demon recounting this; and recognizing his error, he was Baptized and became a monk. From the beginning of his monastic life he maintained humility, saying, "Humility destroys all the power of the enemy, as I myself heard from the Devil, who stated, 'When I provoke some disturbance among monastics and one of them backs down and makes a prostration in order to seek forgiveness, all my power is wiped out immediately.'"

❀   ❀   ❀

Once some people went to the Thebaid to an Elder, taking with them a demonized man for him to cure. The Elder refused, since he did not consider himself worthy; but after they implored him many times, he said to the demon, "Come out of God's creature."

The demon answered, "I am coming out; but I ask you to tell me one thing: who are the goats and who are the sheep?"

"I am the goats," replied the Elder, "and as for the sheep, God knows who they are."

As soon as the demon heard this answer, he cried out with a loud voice, "I am coming out because of your humility"; and at that very moment, he came out of the demonized man.

❈   ❈   ❈

An Elder said that if one humbles himself and says, "Forgive me," to someone, he burns up the demons.

❉   ❉   ❉

If the farmer does not cover the eyes of his beast, it would turn around and devour the fruits of his labors. The same thing happens with us. By God's dispensation we receive coverings for our eyes, lest we see the good deeds that we do and call ourselves blessed, and thereby lose our reward. This is why God allows us from time to time to have unclean thoughts—and we notice only these, in order that we may censure ourselves. For us, these internal pollutions serve to cover our meager goodness; for when a man reproaches himself, then he does not lose his reward.

※　※　※

An Elder was asked, "What is humility?"

He replied, "Humility is a great and Divine work; the path that leads to humility consists in bodily labors and in considering yourself a sinner beneath everyone else."

The brother who had posed the question asked again, "What does it mean to be beneath everyone else?"

The Elder replied, "It means not to be concerned about the sins of others, but only about your own, and to pray to God unceasingly."

❀　❀　❀

There was a brother who lived in the hermits' cells and who had attained to such humility that he always prayed to God, "Lord, send me a thunderbolt; for when I am healthy, I disobey Thee."

❀　❀　❀

A monk, when offended by a certain person, made a prostration to the one who offended him.

❀　❀　❀

In a cœnobion [a community of monks or nuns, as opposed to a community of hermits] there lived a monk who took upon himself all of the burdens of the brethren and who reached the point of accusing himself even of fornication, saying, "I have committed this sin."

Some of the monks, who were not aware of his virtue, began to murmur against him and to say, "See how many evil things he does, and he works no good."

The Abbot, who was familiar with the deeds of this monk, said to his accusers, "I prefer a single rush-mat plaited by him with humility to all yours that you plait with pride. If you like,

I will give you proof of it from God." He ordered a fire to be lighted and had each monk bring three rush-mats that he had plaited; as well, he asked the accused monk for one of his mats. He then commanded that the mats be thrown into the fire. As soon as they were thrown into the fire, all those made by the accusers were burned, while that of the accused brother was not.

When his former accusers saw this miracle, they were frightened and made a prostration to the monk whom they had accused, thereafter honoring him as a Father.

\* \* \*

Abba Longinos was once asked, "Which is the greatest of all the virtues?"

He replied, "I reckon that just as pride is the greatest of the passions, since it was able to cast various beings down from Heaven, so also is humility the greatest of all the virtues. For it has the power to raise a man up from those dark abysses, even if he is a sinner like the Devil. This is why the Lord called the poor in spirit, that is, the humble, blessed above all others."

# CHAPTER 2

# OBEDIENCE

For forty years Abba Doulas lived in a monastic brotherhood, where he was, it is said, a perfect example of a good, obedient monk. He then later went into the desert and became a hermit. With the rich experiences which he had acquired, he was in a position to give sound advice to the younger monks.

"I have tested all of the styles of monastic life," he would tell them, "and have found that monks living together in a monastery make greater progress in acquiring virtue if they are willing to place themselves under the yoke of obedience."

\* \* \*

A certain brother asked of Saint Paisios: "What can I do, Abba, since my heart is hard and I do not fear God?"

"Go and submit yourself to the obedience of an Elder who has fear of God," the Saint counselled him. "In his presence, you too will learn to fear God."

\* \* \*

"Obedience, together with temperance, brings even wild beasts into subjection," said Anthony the Great.

\* \* \*

"Come, my child, and taste of the blessed life of obedience," Abba Moses said to a young man who was readying himself to follow the monastic life. "In obedience you will find humility, strength, joy, patience, and forbearance. From it, contrition is born and love blossoms. It aids the good disciple in keeping all of the Divine commandments the whole of his life."

\* \* \*

Abba Hyperechios also calls obedience the monk's invaluable treasure. Whoever attains to it, let him be assured that his prayer will always be heard and that it will be presented boldly before the throne of Him Who was obedient even unto death.

❀   ❀   ❀

Again, Abba Rouphos says that greater glory awaits a monk in obedience to a spiritual Father than the hermit who lives by his own will in the solitude of the desert.

❀   ❀   ❀

"Three things are especially pleasing to God," says Abba Joseph the Thebite. "Illness endured with patience; work done without recognition, solely for love of Him; and obedience rendered to a spiritual Father with total self-denial. This last feat is most splendidly crowned."

❀   ❀   ❀

"Do not be misled into thinking that you are able to govern yourself in things spiritual," advised Abba Poimen. "Submit yourself to an experienced Elder and let him guide you in all things."

❀   ❀   ❀

Another Father gave this advice to those who had decided to follow the life of obedience: "Become, brother, like the camel. Bearing your imperfections, let your spiritual guide, who knows the way better than you, direct you on the path of God."

❀   ❀   ❀

Four monks from afar once went to consult Saint Pambo. The first was a great faster, the second utterly poor, the third had devoted himself to serving the aged and the infirm, and the fourth had spent twenty years in obedience to his Elder.

Hearing of their virtues, the Saint told them these words: "This last monk here has surpassed all of you, since you others, in all that you do, do it according to your own wills. But since he daily sacrifices his own will, undoubtedly his heart bleeds. It is for this reason that monks who are good in obedience are numbered among the confessors of the Faith."

❧ ❧ ❧

One of the ancient and great Elders, while he was praying one day, entered into ecstasy and ascended in spirit to the heavenly world. There he beheld four distinct ranks of the righteous. In the first rank were assigned those who had suffered bodily illnesses during their lives and had endured them without complaint, thanking God. In the second were all those who had practiced the virtue of love and who had in every way comforted their fellow man. The third rank was comprised of hermits and anchorites, who had lived with extreme suffering and hardship. The fourth was composed of all those who had lived in obedience. These last were shown to surpass all of the others in glory. As a sign of their high rank, they were wearing pure gold cuffs.

"How does it happen that these, the least, have greater glory than the rest?" the Elder asked the Angel who had escorted him.

"Because all of the others," the Angel explained, "lived according to their own wills, whereas these sacrificed their wills daily for the love of God, continually crucifying themselves."

❋ ❋ ❋

Two brothers, out of love for Christ, left the world and pursued the monastic life. One became a hermit. The other chose the sure yoke of submission to save his soul and become a paradigm of obedience. He willingly, and with joy, performed whatever others asked of him and for this reason they loved and revered him.

Once the hermit wanted to test his brother's obedience, to confirm that all that was said of him was true. So, one day he took his brother on a short walk and purposely misled him to the river, which was filled with crocodiles.

"Jump in and get out on the other side," he ordered his brother, as they drew near, certain that he would never do it, since the crocodiles would eat him.

However, the obedient brother, without a thought of doubt in his mind, jumped into the river and crossed to the other shore. Not a single mishap befell him. The beasts, becoming tame, licked his feet. The hermit saw all of this and marvelled.

As they started to return to the monastery, they encountered a naked corpse.

"Let us get a piece of cloth to cover him," the hermit suggested.

"Should we not rather pray," the obedient monk replied. "Perhaps God will resurrect him."

Both of them stood in prayer and, indeed, the dead man resurrected. The hermit attributed this to himself.

"Undoubtedly, my great asceticism produced this miracle," he thought to himself.

However, as they approached the monastery, the Abbot, who was a holy man, and to whom God had revealed all of these things, lost no time in delivering the hermit from his delusion.

"Why did you expose your brother to such danger?" he told the hermit reprovingly. "But note how, by virtue of his obedience, the dead man was resurrected."

The hermit recognized his error and asked forgiveness from God and from his brother.

❄   ❄   ❄

A young monk went to seek the advice of a certain spiritual Elder.

"I perform all of my monastic duties," he told the Elder, "and even more besides. Yet my soul is not at rest. I receive no consolation from God."

"You are living by your own will—for this reason all of this befalls you," the Elder explained to him.

"What should I then do, Abba, in order to find rest?"

"Go find an Elder who has fear of God in his soul. Surrender yourself to him in all that he wishes and allow him to guide you, according to *his* knowledge, on the path of God. Then your soul will find consolation."

The young monk heeded the advice of the Elder and his soul found rest.

❖ ❖ ❖

Abba Mark, the hermit, gives this useful advice to young people who wish to walk the road of obedience: "Do not become the disciple of one who is used to praising himself, lest, instead of learning humility, you learn pride."

❀ ❀ ❀

"I have known monks," Saint Anthony the Great, the boast of the desert, once said, "who after tremendous toil and ascetic struggle fell into sin and lost their reason. The cause of their fall was the faith they had acquired in themselves and in their works. These unfortunate monks forgot the wise counsel of the Scriptures: 'Ask thy father and he will show it thee; thine Elders and they will tell thee'" [Deuteronomy 32:7].

Yet another time he said: "A good disciple must tell his Elder how many steps he takes and how many droplets of water he has drunk, lest he err in these things also."

❖ ❖ ❖

The disciple of a certain Elder found a beautiful place deep in the desert which was ideal for a hermitage.

"Permit me, Abba," he told the Elder, "to go and stay there, in that I expect much gain therefrom."

"It is not a location which offers gain to a man," the wise Elder answered him, "but the way that he lives. The young first need obedience in order to progress."

❀ ❀ ❀

Abba Moses the Black was of the same opinion. "A neophyte monk," he said, "who has not learned obedience and humility, but fasts and does ascetic labors on his own, one should not expect to make progress. Such a monk has not the slightest idea what it means to be a monk."

❀   ❀   ❀

"A virtue which a monk acquires on his own," says Abba Theonas, "one should not expect to stay with him for any great time. God takes His Grace from him, since He knows that the monk will be misled into trusting only in himself. Permanent virtue one finds in those blessed disciples who have given over themselves in body and soul to their spiritual Father."

❀   ❀   ❀

It is said of Abba John the Cripple that, before he became a hermit, he lived many years in obedience to a certain Elder in the Thebaid. When he first arrived, in order to test him his Abba fetched him one day. After having walked some twelve hours distant from their hut, they arrived at a dry spot. The Elder then took his staff, drove it into the ground, and ordered the young John to go every day with a bucket of water to irrigate it. The young disciple willingly fulfilled the command of his Elder. After three years, the dry piece of wood sprouted and bore walnuts. So, the Elder picked them and took them to the church on Sunday. After the Liturgy, he distributed them to the hermits, saying to them: "Come, brothers, and taste of the fruits of obedience."

❀   ❀   ❀

A certain layman from the Thebaid went to the skete of Abba Sisoes and asked the Abba to make him a monk.

"Did you leave any close relatives in the world?" the Elder asked him.

"Yes, Abba, a son."

"First, go throw him in the river and afterwards come to me, so that I can make you a monk," Abba Sisoes told him.

Without hesitation the man left to carry out his obedience. The Saint, however, sent his disciple to follow behind the man to prevent him from such an act. He caught up with the man, who was ready to throw his son in the river, just in time to stop him.

"Do not prevent me from this, brother," the man told him. "This is an obedience from my Abba."

The brother then explained to him that it was in this way that the Elder had wanted to test him and, after some difficulty, convinced the man. As soon as they returned to the skete, Abba Sisoes immediately made him a monk, since he showed himself a perfect disciple.

❀ ❀ ❀

A young man, wellborn and of wealth, found in himself the desire to follow the hermit's life. He searched and found the most austere Elder of the desert, asking that the Elder place him under his obedience.

"Go first and distribute all that you have to the poor," the Elder advised him, "that you might fulfill the commandment of Christ. And afterwards I will accept you."

The young man willingly did as the Abba told him and, being less burdened by material cares, he returned.

"Now you will live in that cell," the Elder ordered him, "never speaking with anyone."

For five whole years the young man struggled in his cell and not a word came forth from his mouth. The other brothers, seeing his reverence and his patience, revered and honored him. One day his Elder called the young man to his cell and told him austerely: "I see how you not only are not profiting by staying in this place, but that you are in danger of losing your soul from praises that are given to you by the brothers, of which you are, indeed, unworthy. Get yourself ready to leave Egypt. I am going to send you to a large monastery where the monks live in common."

The good disciple, again without letting a word come forth from his mouth, lowered his head, in order to show his submission, and immediately prepared himself for the long journey. His Elder gave him a letter of introduction for the Abbot of the large monastery, asking that the Abbot accept the disciple, but forgetting to tell the Abbot whether the disciple would be allowed to speak or not, there where he was going. Thus the young man, faithfully keeping the command of his Elder, did not open his mouth to give forth speech there where he went. Most took him for a mute. The Abbot of the monastery, in order to be sure of this, sent him one day, when he knew the river was flooding, to cross to the opposite bank. It will be necessary for him to return and to tell me that he could not cross, he reckoned. He sent another brother behind him to see what the young man would do.

When the disciple reached the river and saw that it could not be crossed, he knelt and prayed. A crocodile then appeared from out of the river and stood in front of him. The young man climbed up on its back and the beast took him to the other side.

The brother who had followed him returned in amazement to the monastery to relate all that had taken place before his eyes. From that day forth, the Abbot and all the brothers revered the young man as a saint.

After no more than a few years, the good disciple died and the Abbot wrote to the disciple's Elder: "Even though you sent us a mute man, he yet lived among us like an Angel." How surprised the Abbot was, however, when the Elder answered him that this blessed man was not a mute at all, but, because of his spiritual father's command, had remained so many years speechless!

\*    \*    \*

An Elder had a disciple so willing in obedience that he performed immediately and exactly what the Elder told him to do. One day the Abba, in order to test him, told him to get the book that was being read in the church and to throw it into the lighted furnace. Without hesitation, the disciple did as his Elder bid him.

But, because of his obedience, just as the book was thrown into the fire, the fire at once went out.

❀    ❀    ❀

A father once took his young son and went into the desert to become a monk. He became the disciple of a wise Elder. The Elder, in order to test his obedience, one day, just as the disciple kindled the oven in order to bake bread, called to him to throw his young son in. The good disciple, without delaying, grabbed his child and threw him into the fire. But because of the disciple's obedience, the fire formed an arch around the boy and left him completely untouched.

❀    ❀    ❀

Saint Poimen, learning that Abba Nisthero, from a neighboring monastery, was a paradigm of good discipleship, went there to confirm this with his own eyes. He saw, indeed, not only that Nisthero was perfect in his obedience to his Elder, but that he was patient in trials and had attained to great silence.

"How did you acquire such great virtues, brother?" Saint Poimen prevailed upon him to confess.

"When I first came to the monastery, Abba, I thought to myself: You and the horse who turn the mill, my humble one, are one and the same thing. They beat the horse, compel it to work and to bear burdens, and abuse it; yet it does not complain. 'Do the same,' I told myself. Moreover, did not even the Psalmist say, 'I became as a beast before Thee, and I am ever with Thee' [Psalm 72:21]?"

❀    ❀    ❀

"Do you wish to save your soul, brother?" Abba Poimen would tell his disciples. " Then become like a stone pillar. Neither become angry when you are abused nor proud-minded when you are praised."

❀　❀　❀

For twelve years Abba Ammoes was tortured by an illness. Through this whole period, John, his good disciple, stood by him like a lighted torch and served him in every way. The Elder was strict and never said a sweet word to his disciple, not even, "May you be saved." But in his final moments, when all of his fellow ascetics had gathered around, the Elder, with emotion, took into his trembling hands the hands of his disciple, kissed them, and whispered: "My child, you may be certain that you are saved on account of your good obedience."

Afterwards he turned to the fathers and, pointing at John, said to them: "This one that you are looking at is an Angel, not a man."

❀　❀　❀

"Monks under obedience," Abba Isidore said, "have a duty to love their Elders even as fathers and to fear them even as lords. Neither do they ignore fear for the sake of love nor sully love by fear."

❀　❀　❀

John, the disciple of Abba Paul, was a model of obedience. The Fathers relate the following incident regarding him:

Not far from their hut there was a cave in which a hyena had made its lair. One day the Elder saw that there were some wild onions growing around the cave and sent John to pick them, so that they could cook them.

"What should I do, Abba, if the hyena happens to come out?" the young monk asked.

"Tie him up and bring him here," the Elder said in jest.

His good disciple went out to fulfill the command of his Elder. But just as he had anticipated, the fierce beast suddenly attacked him. Not only did the youth not show cowardice, but he rushed to tie the beast up. Then this strange thing took place: instead of the monk being afraid, the beast became afraid and ran into the desert to save itself.

John chased behind it and called out: "Stop, now! My Abba ordered me to tie you up."

Later, after much effort, he caught up with the hyena, tied it up, and took it to his Elder. The Elder, in the meanwhile, having become uneasy, seeing that the disciple was late, had gone out in order to meet him. Thus he saw him coming, dragging behind him the bound beast, and marvelled at the power of obedience.

To John, however, he showed no surprise at all. Indeed, on the contrary, in order to humble him, he yelled at him, supposedly harshly: "Stupid, why did you bring this rabid dog here?"

He then unleashed the wild beast and let it go free to return to its cave.

❀　❀　❀

Saint Basil the Great once went to visit a monastery in his province and, having instructed the monks for many hours, afterwards turned to the Abbot and asked him: "Is there to be found one among the brothers who has acquired the virtue of obedience?"

"We are all servants of Your Holiness," said the Abbot, "and we strive for the salvation of our souls."

"Is there anyone who stands out because of his obedience?" the Hierarch persisted in asking.

The Abbot then pointed out a young monk and ordered him to serve the Saint as long as he was staying in the monastery. After the meal, the young monk took a vessel of water to the Saint and poured it out so that he could wash his hands. When the Bishop was finished washing, he took the pitcher in his hands and offered to pour the water for the monk so that he, too, could wash. The monk, without objection or false humility, accepted.

"In the morning when I enter the church to liturgize," the Saint said to him, "remind me to ordain you a Deacon."

On the next day, the good disciple did just as he had been ordered.

"This monk shows true obedience," the Saint said to the Abbot, "and he will progress without fail."

Hence, he ordained him Deacon and Presbyter and took him with him to serve him.

❀    ❀    ❀

Abba Silouan was the Abbot of a small monastery on top of Mount Sinai, where he had twelve monks in all. Among them, one young monk, who was of aristocratic background and who had sacrificed everything for the love of Christ, stood out because of his absolute obedience. On account of his virtues, the young man had become greatly beloved by Abba Silouan. The other monks, however, were envious of Mark—so the good youth was named—and complained to the Fathers of Sinai that their Elder showed him special consideration.

So the other Fathers went to censure Abba Silouan.

"Come," the holy Elder humbly told them, "to confirm for yourselves what it is that Mark does to distinguish himself from the others."

He took them and they made a round of the entire monastery. They stopped outside each cell, knocked on the door, and called to each brother by name. From within, the voice of each was heard: "Now, at once, Abba." But no one would appear.

Then shortly: "At this moment I cannot come out. I am busy."

Yet again at another cell: "In just a moment, Abba, as soon as I finish the strand of reeds I am braiding."

Finally, they came to Mark's cell. Upon hearing the voice of his Elder, the good disciple hurried outside immediately. Abba Silouan found a pretext to send him off and afterwards turned to the fathers: "Where are the other monks whom I called? Not one of them came, except this blessed child of obedience."

They then entered Mark's cell. He had been drawing and had left unfinished a small curve, in order to heed the summons of his Elder.

"He is really worthy of your love," the Fathers said to Abba Silouan. "From this day he will also have our favor and respect, for God loves him and has favored him."

*   *   *

Another time, the Fathers were walking with Abba Silouan in the desert. Not far behind Mark and the other brothers were coming. The Elder, in order to show the other Fathers the absolute obedience of his disciple, called Mark near and, pointing out to him a snail that was crawling a short distance ahead of them, said: "My child, do you see that buffalo?"

"Yes, Abba," he answered.

"Do you also see his horns, which look to be double-sized?"

"Yes, Abba," said Mark, who saw only with the eyes of his Elder.

And so yet another time the Fathers of Sinai found occasion to marvel at the devoted disciple.

*   *   *

There was an elderly hermit who fell to laziness, neglected his duties, and, along with other evil things, acquired the habit of drinking and becoming drunk. All day long he wove baskets in his hut. As soon as the sun went down, however, he went to the nearest village, delivered his handiwork, and remained until early morning in the tavern.

Once a young man came from afar to the hermit and asked him to make him a monk and place him under obedience. The lazy Elder did not hesitate, keeping the young man and teaching him also to weave baskets. Thus, he had more to spend on the cursed drink. He began to drink twice as much as before and to exploit mercilessly the labor of the brother. In the mornings he would come staggering to his cell, carrying a little dry bread in his knapsack for his unfortunate disciple.

Three whole years went by in this way. The brother passed through great privations—he had insufficient bread and his clothes hung from him in tatters. Yet he endured without grumbling and never complained to his Elder.

One time, however, his thoughts began to war against him: "Of what benefit is this man to me?" he reflected. "He wastes the products of my work, showing no pity, and I am about to die from starvation. Why do I stay, then, and not flee from here?"

Even though right was wholly on his side, he courageously resisted these thoughts.

"Where would you go?" he said to himself. "Did you not promise your Lord that you would endure all trials?"

As he was struggling thus, an Angel, sent by God, appeared before him to bring him a joyful message: "Do not leave, brother. Tomorrow a host of us will come to fetch you."

The next day the disciple said to his Elder: "Do not leave the cell this evening, Abba, because those who will take me away are coming."

The old hermit promised, but as his drinking hour approached, he was in no way able to restrain himself. He began to doubt the words of his disciple: "It looks to me as though they are not coming today. Do you not see how late they are? Maybe they changed their minds," he told the disciple caustically, starting for the door.

"Look, they are coming, Abba," the young man called out joyfully. Just as he said this, he crossed his hands over his chest and gave up his soul.

The old hermit remained stunned for hours by this sudden happening. Afterwards, he came to his senses and, weeping bitterly over his evil state, spoke to his disciple as though he were standing alive before him: "Alas am I, a wretch, having passed my life in laziness. You, my child, for a little patience saved your soul."

But from then on he once and for all cut off his bad habit and resolved to pass the remainder of his life in temperance and diligence.

❀   ❀   ❀

There once lived a hermit in the environs of Alexandria. A man of callous character, irascible and fussy, it was impossible for anyone to live with him. But a pious young man, who had a desire to be a monk, hearing of the Elder's bad reputation, made the following contract with God: "Lord," he said in prayer, "in order that you might forgive all of the sins which I have committed since my youthful years, I am going voluntarily to this hermit, and I promise to remain in submission to him to the end."

So he said and so he did. He submitted to the callous Elder and each day accepted, without complaint, his eccentricities, abuses and humiliations, and unimaginable maltreatment.

After some six years, God, seeing the disciple's patience, sent him consolation from Heaven. In his sleep, he saw an Angel of the Lord holding a large ledger, of which half was completely erased and the other half was filled with writing.

"Half of your debt has been discharged," the Angel told him, showing him the ledger. "Now all you need do is work on the balance."

Another spiritual Elder, who was leading an ascetic life nearby, followed the struggles of the brother with sympathy and had become close friends with him. Whenever he heard the eccentric Elder abuse him and hit him, the Elder would lovingly ask him: "How did your day go, child? Did it profit you anything? Did you erase any lines from the ledger?"

If at times—this happened very rarely—his Elder did not abuse or beat him, the brother would sadly go to his good neighbor and complain to him: "A bad day today, Abba. It passed in peace. It brought me no profit."

After six more years of tormented life, the brother reposed. It was revealed to the spiritual Elder that he was numbered among the holy Martyrs and that he interceded boldly before God for his Abba.

"Lord," he would say, "just as, because of him, you were merciful to *me,* have mercy on *him* because of Thy great mercies."

The prayer of the patient disciple was heard. The hard-hearted Elder repented, changed his life, and his soul was saved.

※  ※  ※

One of the great Fathers of the Desert once reflected: "I wonder to what measure of holiness I have attained?" But our good God, in order to protect him from haughtiness, revealed to him that in a neighboring monastery there lived a certain monk much higher than he in virtue, but who nonetheless considered himself very sinful and the least among all.

So the Elder set out one day to visit the monastery. He asked the Abbot to see all of the monks. The Abbot immediately gave the order that all of the monks appear before the Saint. The Elder observed each one with care, but was not satisfied. He did not see among them the monk whom God had revealed to him.

"There must be another brother in the monastery," he said to the Abbot.

"Yes," he said, "there is another one, but he is a little simple of mind and works in the fields."

"Bring him, too," the Saint requested.

They hastily led the brother to the Elder. As soon as the Elder saw him, he embraced him and kissed him, for he knew him from his face, which God had shown him. He afterwards took him aside and asked him to tell him what his secret labor was.

"I do nothing, Abba," the brother said, "I am an ignorant man, as you see."

But the Elder was not about to let him go unless he revealed to him his virtue. So, the brother was obliged to trust him.

"My Elder, Abba, many years ago, when I came to the monastery, put the monastery ox in the cell where I work and sleep. Every day it would crush my weaving. For thirty years I endured this suffering, and not even one time did I allow myself to entertain a bad thought about my Abba. Nor did I ever tie up the animal. I always began my weaving again, thanking God for this little temptation."

The Saint marvelled at the patience of this good disciple and from it also understood the rest of his virtues.

❀   ❀   ❀

A young monk, going down from his skete to the city, passed by the cell of Abba Ammoun and confessed to him: "My Elder, Abba, is sending me to the city to do some work. But I, who am a man with weaknesses, fear temptations."

"Do obedience," the Saint advised him, "and if temptation befalls you, say these words: 'O God of powers, through the prayers of my father, rescue me.'"

The brother took courage from the words of the Abba and went willingly to his duty. The Devil, however, who bided his time in order to harm the brother, hurled at him a fallen woman to lure him into her iniquitous den. In his distress, the young man remembered suddenly the words of Abba Ammoun and cried with faith: "O God of powers, through the prayers of my father, rescue me."

He then found himself, without knowing how, on the road which led to the desert.

❀   ❀   ❀

Abraham, the disciple of Abba Sisoes, told the brothers how he once had a great struggle with the flesh. His Elder, seeing him unsettled and sad, understood this, and, raising his hands toward Heaven, prayed these words: "Lord, Thou who wishest not the death of a sinner, have mercy on thy servant and rescue him from temptation."

Even before the Saint had lowered his hands, the young man had been completely delivered from his struggle.

❀   ❀   ❀

The disciple of a certain Elder went to fetch water from the well, which was about three hours distant from their hut. When he arrived there, he remembered that he had not taken the rope with him.

"Lord, help me in my need, through the prayers of my holy Elder," the young man prayed, having faith in God and trust in the prayers of his Abba.

With surprise he then saw the water rise to the rim of the well. When he had filled his vessels, the water again descended to its normal depth.

❊   ❊   ❊

The disciple of another Elder suffered greatly from fleshly desires and, not being able any longer to resist, returned to the world and found a woman to marry.

His Elder was inconsolable because of the brother's fall and implored God to shelter him, lest he lose the chastity which he had vowed when he became a monk. God heard the prayer of his servant and deemed that the brother die, without having been polluted, on the very day he had set for his marriage.

❊   ❊   ❊

There lived an Elder with his disciple in a hut in the Thebaid. Every evening after *Apodeipnon* [Compline], the Abba called his disciple to him to hear his confession and, at the end, gave him his blessing to go to sleep.

One day it happened that many visitors came to consult the Elder. He remained with them the whole day, instructing them and refreshing their souls. When it fell dark and the visitors left, though he was tired out, the Elder did not fail to call his disciple to their customary duties. As he was talking to him, however, being exhausted, the Elder fell into a deep sleep. The young disciple remained fixed in his place, with his hands folded on his chest, waiting for his Elder to wake up and give him a blessing to go to bed. But the Elder did not wake up. The night progressed. The brother began to get tired and dozed off. He thought of leaving without a blessing, but each time decided not to. The middle of the night came and he had, up to then, seven times been tempted by his thoughts to give up and to leave. But he courageously resisted them.

Finally, as dawn began to break, the Elder suddenly awoke and, seeing his disciple standing in the same place, was astonished.

"Have you not gone to lie down yet?" he asked him.

"No, Abba, you did not give me a blessing."

"Why did you not wake me, my child?"

"I felt sorry for you, since you were so tired."

They said the morning service together and the Elder sent the young monk to rest for a short time. The Elder continued his prayer. But suddenly he fell into ecstasy and saw before him a Divine Angel, who took him by the hand and led him to a place which was indescribable in its beauty. There the Angel showed him a throne that was shining with heavenly light. Above it were seven crowns of pure gold.

"To whom do these belong?" the Elder asked in wonderment.

"To your disciple," answered the Angel. "The place and the throne of God have been ready for him long before, on account of his perfect obedience. But the gold crowns he earned all at once on this night."

When the Elder came to himself, he called his disciple and examined him about his thoughts the preceding night, when he had remained awake.

The young man wracked his brains for some time, but finally remembered: "Seven times, my Abba, my thoughts warred with me, so as to tempt me to go to bed without a blessing. But I resisted them and finally did not go."

The Elder was amazed at the patient endurance of his disciple, but did not reveal to him his vision, so as not to bring him harm. To his other disciples, however, he often related it, in order to provide them with a good example.

⁂

## CHAPTER 3

# REPENTANCE

A brother lived in a cell in Egypt and, with all humility, spent his life in asceticism. This monk had a sister who lived in the city and who was a prostitute. She had been the cause of many losing their souls each day. Thus, many times the Elders had urged the brother to go meet with his sister. At last one day they convinced him to go, that perchance his brotherly admonitions might have the desired effect and she might cease the sin that she was committing.

As soon as he arrived at the place where the sinful woman was staying, a certain acquaintance of theirs saw the monk and ran to inform her, saying: "Your brother is asking for you at the door below." The sister, on hearing this news, abandoned her sinful compatriots and, just as she was, ran down to greet her brother, without bothering, in fact, even to put a covering on her head. When the brother and sister saw one another and she, out of joy, tried to embrace her brother, he said: "Truly, my sister, I pity your soul, beholding how you will suffer the bitter and unending torments of Hell; for not only have you lost your soul, but many others have also done so because of you."

The sister listened attentively to the sincere counsels of her brother and, overwhelmed by them, with true repentance said to him: "Are you sure that, even now, I can be saved?"

"If you wish so, there is salvation," the kind brother answered with certainty.

With tears in her eyes, she then fell at the feet of her brother and doggedly entreated him to take her with him into the desert to be saved.

The brother, also moved by her sudden conversion, told his sister: "Put a scarf on your head and follow me."

She, however, said to her brother: "Come, come, let us go quickly. It is preferable for me, and better for my soul, if I leave this vile place and set forth on the way bare-headed, and not enter again into this workshop of sin."

They thus departed for the desert, and the brother advised her tenderly, enumerating for her the fruits of repentance. She listened with silent attention, while Divine Grace slowly won over the soul of the repentant sinner.

Then at a certain point in their journey, they saw some wayfarers coming toward them from the opposite direction. So the brother, in order not to cause scandal to them, told his sister: "Since not everyone knows that you are my sister, get off the road just a little until these people pass by, so that we do not cause them scandal."

The sister immediately went away some distance from the road. When the caravan had passed, the brother called to his sister. But he received no answer at all. Curious, he searched the place where he expected her to be and, astonished, saw that she was dead. He noticed at the same time that her feet were torn to pieces from the trip, since she was barefoot.

The brother related these incidents to the Elders. They, taking counsel regarding the matter, all disagreed, some maintaining that she was saved, others insisting that she had lost her soul.

Finally, after praying, one of the Elders, who appears to have been more virtuous and insightful than the others, received the following revelation from God: "This sinner was saved, for as soon as Divine Grace, at the counsels of her brother, moved her heart, she repented and thought of no material thing. But rather, she gave no heed to her body and did not complain about the pain and wounds inflicted by the journey. For this reason, her repentance was accepted."

✳   ✳   ✳

The parents of a young girl by the name of Taisia died and left her an orphan. The young woman converted her home into a guest house for the Fathers of a neighboring skete. For many years she thus welcomed them and showed them care through her hospitality.

After some time, however, having spent all that she had in her hospitable work for the Fathers, she fell into need and became poor.

So it was that she fell in with some perverted people who led her to change her way of life and to abandon the path of virtue. The result of these destructive associations of hers was that Taisia flourished ever more in the way of sin, ending up, in time, in prostitution.

When the Fathers heard of her plight, it much saddened them.

So, they called upon Abba John the Short and said to him: "We have learned that our sister Taisia is living in sin. It is well known that, when she was still able, she showed us her love and hospitality and gave us rest. It is now time for us to help her as much as we can. Take upon yourself the task, then, of meeting with her and try, with the wisdom that God has given you, to set her aright and to pull her out of the mud of debauchery."

The Elder thus went to the den of sin where Taisia was staying.

"Inform your mistress, please, that I am asking for her," he told the old woman who was the doorkeeper of the house of ill repute.

"Get out of here, monk," the old woman told him angrily. "You monks early on took all that she had and have left her poor now."

"Please go and do as I asked you," the Elder insisted, "because I aim to bring her great benefit."

The old woman finally stubbornly went upstairs and yelled to Taisia that some monk wanted to visit her.

"Those monks," Taisia thought, on hearing who it was who was asking for her, "frequently live near the Red Sea and find valuable pearls."

Having adorned herself with special care, she lay down on her bed and said to the old woman porter: "Bring the monk to me."

So, in fact, shortly Abba John entered the appointed room and sat near her. Looking carefully into her face, he said emotionally: "What is it that you have against Jesus, and why do you blame Him for coming to such a state as this?"

She, upon hearing these words, was totally paralyzed. At the same time, the Elder lowered his head and began to weep in sobs.

Shaken, Taisia then asked him: "Abba, why are you crying?"

Abba John, raising his head a little, and then lowering it again, said: "How can I see Satan playing on your face and not cry?"

At this remark, the sinful Taisia asked: "Is there such a thing as repentance, Father?"

"Yes, there is," the Elder replied.

"Then take me with you," Taisia said, "and direct me as you will."

"So, let us go now."

At the beckoning of the Elder, the repentant sinner immediately arose to follow him. The Elder was beset by astonishment, since he saw that Taisia had no interest in settling her household matters, but left things just as they were and followed him.

By the time they reached the desert, it had become completely dark. Abba John prepared a little place to sleep for her and, having made the sign of the Cross on it, told her: "Sleep here." And after he had prepared for himself an improvised place to sleep on the ground, a short distance away, he completed his prayers and lay down to rest.

During the middle of the night he awakened and saw a strange spectacle; he saw a shining pathway leading heavenward from the spot where Taisia was sleeping and Angels of God leading the soul of the repentant sinner upwards along it.

Immediately he got up and, rushing toward Taisia, tapped her lightly with his foot. Once he realized that she was indeed dead, he prostrated with his face to the earth and entreated God to reveal to him whether He had accepted Taisia's repentance. Praying in this manner, he heard a voice from God, which said to him: "The single hour for which this women repented was more quickly received than that of many who spend years in repentance, since the repentance of the latter is not as earnest as hers."

❊    ❊    ❊

There once lived in the city, it was said, a young man who committed many and frightful sins. However, this young man was piercingly censured by his conscience, on account of his manifold sins, and, with the help of God, came to repentance. Under the power of repentance, he went to a cemetery, where he established himself in one of the tombs and lamented for his former life, falling down with his face to the earth and continually groaning from the depths of his heart.

When he had passed a week in this state of unrelenting and persistent repentance, demons, who had before brought his life to destruction, gathered around one night making noise and shouting: "Who is this impious man, who used to pass his time in lustful things and immorality and now wants us to think that he is sober and a doer of good deeds? And he wants to be a Christian and become virtuous, now that he can no longer have fun and fulfill his pleasures? What good can he expect in his life, since he is filled with our evils?

"Hey you! Will you not get up from there at all? Will you not come with us to your customary places of sin and depravity? Fallen women and wine await you; will you not come to indulge your desires? After all the sins that you have committed up to this day, all hope for salvation is lost to you, and therefore, O struggler, you will only march on full speed to your damnation if you continue killing yourself this way. Why are you so intent and in such a hurry to be damned? Whatever transgression that there is, you committed it; together with us, you fell to every sin. Yet now you dare to flee our company? Do you not agree? Will you not go along with our offers?"

Meanwhile, however, the young man persisted in the sorrow of repentance and, appearing not to hear the exhortations of the demons, did not answer them at all. So the demons, seeing that they had accomplished nothing with their words, fell upon him, beat him cruelly, and, when they had wounded him all over, left him half-dead. But still the youth remained immovable in his place, groaning, and steadfast in his obdurate repentance.

During this time, the young man's relatives sought him out, finally finding him. Having learned the reason for his appearance—that is, of the brazen attack of the demons—, they tried to take him with them to their home. He, however, refused to abandon the place of his repentance.

The following night, the demons again attacked him and tormented him even more greatly. His relatives visited him for a second time, though without persuading him to leave his place of punishment and follow them. To their proposals on the matter, he answered patiently and with resignation: "Do not pressure me. I prefer to die than to return to my former prodigal life."

The third night he almost died from the cruel torments of the demons, who attacked him with greater severity than all of the other times.

After that, the demons, having accomplished nothing with their threats and torments—for the young man would not change his mind at any scare tactic—, departed and left him alone.

Fleeing from him, they cried madly: "He conquered us! He conquered us! He conquered us!"

From that time on, nothing bad happened to the youth; rather, with a clean conscience he came to realize every virtue. Until the end of his life, he remained in the tomb, which he made his hermitage, coming to be honored by God with the gifts of miraculous doings.

❊ ❊ ❊

Abba Mios was asked by a soldier: "Father, God then accepts the repentance of the sinner?"

The Elder, after counselling him with many instructive words, suddenly asked him: "Tell me, my beloved, when you tear your uniform, do you throw it away?"

"No," the soldier answered, "I sew it and use it anew again."

Then Abba Mios also thoughtfully told him: "If you take pity on your clothing, will not God take pity on His own creation?"

❊ ❊ ❊

A brother asked Abba Poimen: "Father, I committed a great sin. Is it enough for me to repent for three years?"

The Elder answered: "That is too long a period of time."

Those in attendance asked, with a certain curiosity: "Is forty days of repentance a long enough period of repentance?"

To the question of these observers, the Elder answered: "Again, this is too long. It is my opinion that, if a man repents with his whole heart and does not repeat the sin, within three days only God will accept his repentance and forgive him."

❀   ❀   ❀

Yet another brother asked Abba Poimen: "If someone falls to some sin and repents, does God forgive him?"

Most pensively, Abba Poimen answered: "Would not He who gave to men the commandment that they must forgive, Himself fulfill this? It is well known that He gave an order to the Apostle Peter to forgive those who do wrong and repent, even seven times seventy."

❀   ❀   ❀

And a third brother asked Abba Poimen: "Father, what is repentance for sin?"

The Elder replied to the brother's inquiry: "Repentance signifies a firm resolution not to return to a sin. For this reason precisely the righteous are called blameless, for they have abandoned sin and have been proven righteous."

❀   ❀   ❀

A certain brother asked Abba Sisoes: "Counsel me, Father, for I have fallen to sin. What am I to do?"

The Elder said to him: "When you fall, get up again."

With bitterness the sinning brother continued: "Ah! Father I got up, yet I fell to the same sin again."

The Elder, so as not to discourage the brother, answered: "Then get up again and again."

The young man asked with a certain despondency: "How long can I do that, Father?"

The Elder, giving him courage, said to the brother: "Until the end of your life, whether you be found in the commendable attempt to lift yourself up from sin or falling again to it. For, wherever it is that a man is found at the last moment of his life on earth, whether it be in things good or evil, there he will be judged, proceeding either to punishment or to reward."

❀  ❀  ❀

A certain brother, overcome by the passion of immorality, sinned every day. However, each time, with tears and prayers, he would fall before the Master and Lord and receive forgiveness from Him. And as soon as he had repented, the next day, being misled again by shameful habit, he would fall to sin.

Afterwards, having sinned, he would go to the Church, where he would prostrate himself before the honorable and revered Icon of our Lord Jesus Christ and tearfully confess to Jesus: "Lord, have mercy upon me and take away from me this fearful temptation, for it troubles me fiercely and wounds me with the bitter taste of the pleasures. O my Master, cleanse my person once more, that I may gaze upon Thine Icon and see Thy holy form and the sight of Thy face, brighter than the sun, that my heart might be sweetened and thankful."

And though his lips had just whispered these words, no sooner would he leave the Church than he would fall once again to sin.

Despite this, however, he did not despair of his salvation, but, returning from his sinful deed, would cry out in the Church the same words to God, to the Lord, Who loves mankind, adding the following: "My Lord, I swear to Thee on my word that I shall no longer commit this sin. Only forgive me, Good and Most Merciful Lord, whatever sins I have committed from the beginning to this moment."

No sooner would he utter these awe-inspiring words, than he would find himself the captive of this evil sin. Let no one cease to marvel at the sweet love of God towards mankind and at His boundless goodness, with which He each day tolerated the uncorrected and evil transgression and ingratitude of the brother. Indeed, God, because of the greatness of His mercy, persistently accepted the repentance of that sinful brother and his inevitable return. For this happened not for one or two or three years, but for more than ten years.

Do you see, my brother, the measureless forbearance and boundless love of the Master? How He continually endures, showing to us kindness, tolerating our terrible transgressions and sins? And what evokes astonishment and wonderment with regard to the rich mercies of God is that He did not become wrathful with the brother in question, though the brother, agreeing not to fall to sin again, continually broke his word.

At any rate, one day when all that we have described again occurred, the brother, having fallen to sin, rushed to the Church, lamenting, groaning, and crying with anguish, to invoke the mercy of God, that He might have compassion on him and take him from the sin of immorality.

No sooner had he called on God, the Lover of man, than the Devil, that evil of old, destroyer of our souls, seeing that he could gain nothing, since whatever he accomplished by sin the brother expunged by his repentance, became infuriated and appeared visibly before the brother. Facing the Icon of Christ, the Devil said to our compassionate Savior: "What will become of the two of us, Jesus Christ? Your sympathy for this sinner defeats me and takes the ground I have gained, since you keep accepting this dissolute man and prodigal who daily mocks you and scorns your authority. Indeed, why is it that you do not burn him up, but, rather, tolerate and put up with him? ...Is it because one day you intend to condemn all of the adulterers and the dissolute and you will destroy all sinners?

"Actually, you are not a just Judge. But by whim your power is sometimes applied leniently and overlooks things. So, while I was cast from the heavens down to the abyss for a little breach of pride, to this fellow here, even though an immoral man and a prodigal, you calmly show your sympathy, just because he throws himself down in front of your Icon.

"In what way can you be called a just Judge, then? For, as I see it, you receive individual people with great kindness, but ignore justice in general."

The Devil said all of this, poisoned with great bitterness, whilst there poured forth from his nostrils a black flame.

Having said these things, he fell silent. A voice was heard in response, coming forth from the Divine sanctuary, saying the following: "O all-cunning and ruinous Dragon, are you yet not satisfied with your evil and destructive desire to gobble up the world? Now you have even the nerve to try to do away with this man here, who has come with contrition to entreat the mercy of My compassion—to devour him, too? Can you offer up enough sins that, by them, you can tilt the balance of justice against the precious blood which I shed on the Cross for this man? Behold My murder and death, which I endured for the forgiveness of his sins.

"You, when he turns again to sin, do not turn him away, but receive him with joy, neither chastising him nor preventing him from committing sin, out of the hope that you might win him over; but I, Who am merciful and love mankind, Who counselled My laudable Apostle, Peter, to forgive sins seven times seventy [St. Matthew 18:22], do I not show him mercy and compassion? Indeed, simply because he flees to Me, I will not turn him away until I have won him over. Furthermore, I was crucified for sinners and for their salvation; My immaculate hands were nailed to the Cross, that those who so wish might take refuge in Me and be saved. For this reason, then, I neither turn away nor reject anyone, even if he should fall many times a day and many times return to Me; such a person will not leave My Temple saddened, for I came not to call the righteous, but to call sinners to repent."

During the time that this voice was heard, the Devil was fixed in his place, trembling and unable to run away. The voice then again began to say: "We have heard from all that you say,

O Seducer, that I am not just; to the contrary, I am just beyond all. In whatever moral state I find a person, in that state I judge him. Look at this man who a few moments ago repented, having returned from sin and having fallen at My feet with a sincere resolution to abandon sin, and thereby having conquered you.

"Therefore, I will accept him immediately and save his soul, since he did not lose hope in his hard toil for salvation.

"Look how much he merits by his repentance before Me, for which he is honored. As for you, let your hate be shred to pieces and you disgraced."

While this was being said, the repentant brother had thrown himself before the Icon of the Savior. With his face to the ground and lamenting, he surrendered his spirit to the Lord. At the same time that the repentant brother departed to the Lord, a great tempest fell upon Satan, like a fire from Heaven, and devoured him. From this incident, my brothers, let us learn of the limitless compassion of God and of His love of man—what a good Master we have—, that we might never again be disheartened by our sins, but rather look after our salvation with zeal.

❀   ❀   ❀

Again another brother, having repented of all of the sins that he had committed, attained peace (he no longer fell to any misdeed or sins). It so happened that almost immediately thereafter he stumbled on a rock and injured his foot. So much blood flowed from the wound that he lost consciousness and died. After his death, the demons immediately came, wishing to take his soul.

However, the Angels stopped them and told them: "Look at that rock and see his blood, which he shed in struggle for his love of the Lord."

When they had said this, the Angels ascended with him to Heaven, his soul free of sin.

❀   ❀   ❀

Satan appeared to a brother who had fallen to sin and said to him: "You are not a Christian."

The brother, without being ensnared by this thought of the Devil, answered: "Regardless of what I am today, from now on I will flee from you."

Satan, attempting to cast him into despair, spoke again to him: "I tell you that you are going to Hell."

The brother, not losing his courage, answered a second time: "You are neither my judge nor my God."

So, Satan took leave, having accomplished nothing. The brother then repented sincerely before God and became a valiant struggler.

✳ ✳ ✳

A brother, possessed by sadness and melancholy, went to an Elder and asked of him: "What am I to do? My thoughts present me with the idea that perhaps in vain I denied the world and that I cannot be saved."

Thoughtfully, the Elder answered as follows: "My child, even if we do not succeed in reaching the promised land, it is better that we should give our carcasses to the desert than return to the Egypt of fearful enslavement" [Numbers 14:29–33].

✳ ✳ ✳

Another brother asked the same Elder: "Father, to what does the Prophet refer when he says, 'There is no salvation for him in his God' [Psalm 3:2]?"

The Elder gave the following response to the brother's inquiry: "He is referring to thoughts of despair, which the demons place before the sinner, saying: 'Neither now nor hereafter is it possible for God to save you.' With such counsel they try to cast the sinner into despair. But a person must contrast these thoughts with the words of Holy Scripture: 'The Lord is my refuge and He shall free my feet from the snare' [Psalm 24:15]."

❀   ❀   ❀

One of the Desert Fathers relates the following beneficial story: In Thessaloniki, there was once a convent of virgins. One of the nuns of the convent, by virtue of the works of the Tempter, left the monastery and fell to prostitution. She remained in this loathsome sin of immorality for a number of years. Yet after some time, with the help of God, Who loves mankind, she repented and returned to her convent. But before she was able to enter into the convent, she fell dead at the gates. In the meantime, her death was revealed to a certain holy man. In this revelatory vision, he saw—among other things—the Holy Angels who had come to take her soul and the demons following behind the soul. On the one hand, the Angels claimed that the nun had returned to the convent repentant, and thus her soul belonged to them.

But the demons answered: "She has worked so many years for us, and therefore her soul should be ours. Moreover, she did not even manage to enter into the convent. How, then, can you claim that she repented?"

The Angels, however, cut them off, saying that from the moment that God, Who is omniscient, perceived that the nun's intention was aimed at repentance, He gladly received her and she was justified. "She was master over her repentance, in reaching the goal which she had intended; the Lord over her life, however, was the Master of all."

After hearing these words, the demons were thwarted and departed, leaving the soul to the Angels.

The holy man who beheld this vision related it to others.

❀   ❀   ❀

Abba Alonios said: "If a man but so desires, he can return to the Divine standard and repent anytime, whether early or late."

❀   ❀   ❀

A brother posed the following question to Abba Moses: "Let us suppose that a man beats his servant for a certain transgression; what should the servant say?"

The Elder replied: "If he is a good servant, he will say: 'My Lord, have mercy on me, for I have done wrong.'"

The brother asked again: "Should the servant say nothing else?"

And the Elder answered again: "Nothing else. For, having admitted and confessed his fault and having said, 'I have done wrong,' immediately his Lord will take pity on him from the depth of his soul and forgive him."

\* \* \*

A brother said to Abba Poimen: "When I fall to some deplorable sin, my conscience eats me up and sharply reproaches me because I have fallen to that sin."

The Elder answered the brother as follows: "If, at the very moment that he commits a sin, a person says, 'I have sinned,' his conscience ceases to be troubled."

\* \* \*

Two brothers according to the flesh left the world in order to live the monastic life. One of them had established himself in the monastic life on the Mount of Olives. One day his heart was literally red-hot with piercing contrition; so, he immediately went down to Jerusalem and, when he had come to the ruler of the city, confessed to him all of his sins; at the same time, he entreated the ruler, saying to him: "Punish me, as I have broken the law."

The ruler, amazed at the contrition and repentance of the man confessing to him, reflected a bit and said to the brother: "My man, since you have voluntarily confessed and have sincerely repented, I dare not judge you before God has so done; for, indeed, perhaps He has forgiven you."

After this, the brother departed and himself put chains on his body—on his feet and around his neck—and locked himself in his cell. When anyone would happen to visit him and ask, "Who, Abba, put you in these heavy chains?," he would answer, "The ruler."

Anyway, one day, just before his death, an Angel of the Lord went to him and the chains fell away from him. The next day, when the disciple who served him went into the room and saw the monk free from his chains, he asked him with astonishment: "Who released you from your chains?"

"He Who forgave my sins," the monk answered, adding: "Yesterday an Angel of the Lord appeared to me and said: 'Owing to the patience which you have shown, all of your sins are forgiven.' And then he touched my chains with his finger and they fell off of me immediately." No sooner had the monk recounted this incident than he fell into the sleep of eternity.

❀ ❀ ❀

Another brother lived alone in the Monidia Lavra and unceasingly offered this prayer to God: "Lord, since I have no fear of God, send me a thunderbolt, or some punishment, or illness, or a demon, that my hardened soul might revive and come to know the fear of God." At other times, he would again entreat God, saying: "I know, my Master, that I have sinned before Thee greatly and that my wrong deeds are numberless; thus, I dare not ask for Thy forgiveness. But if it be impossible to forgive me, punish me here and not after in Hell eternal. And if it is possible, give me in the present life a portion of Hell, that my Hell in the other life might be milder. I ask only that Thou wouldest begin my punishment now, O Master, though not with righteous anger or wrath, but with mercy and with clemency."

It is thus that he spent an entire year. During the whole of this time, the monk did not fail to fulfill his work of repentance, entreating God with his whole soul and with fervent tears to forgive him, fasting, holding vigils, submitting his body to various hardships and exhausting his soul through contrition.

Once, while he was sitting on the ground, lamenting as usual for his sins and moaning grievously and loudly, he became drowsy from his great sadness and fell asleep. Almost immediately, Christ appeared to him and said, with a voice full of kindness and care: "What is wrong with you, fellow? Why are you crying so inconsolably?"

The monk recognized Who He was immediately and, terror-stricken with fear and reverence, answered Him: "I fell," the monk answered, trembling.

"Then get up," the manifested Lord answered.

"I cannot, Master, unless Thou givest me Thy hand."

So, the Lord stretched out His hand, grasped the monk, and lifted him up. When the monk had gotten up and stood before the Lord, Who had raised him, he began again to weep and to be overcome by piercing grief.

Once again the Lord, made manifest in this vision, spoke with a peaceful and sweet voice: "Why art thou crying, fellow? Why art thou sad?"

Then the brother again said to the Lord: "Dost Thou not wish for me, Lord, to cry and to be sad since, though I have enjoyed so many good things from Thee, I have nonetheless so saddened Thee?"

With these words, the Lord again stretched out His hand and lightly touched the head of the monk, saying to him: "Be not further sad, for, since thou hast suffered such sadness for My sake, I shall bear no sadness on thine account. If I have shed My blood for thee, should I not all the more offer up forgiveness to thee and to every soul which has sincerely repented for his sins?"

No sooner had the brother come out of this blessed vision than he felt his heart full of joy. And, indeed, his inner thoughts revealed to him that God had shown compassion on him. The rest of his years, therefore, he lived in great humility, thanking God for the forgiveness of his sins.

❀   ❀   ❀

An Elder said: "If you fall to a sin and, having recovered from it, set out to grieve and repent for your fall, take care not to cease showing your grief and to sigh to God until death, since there is the danger that you might otherwise fall again to the same sin. Sorrow according to God is a bridle for the soul which will keep you from falling once more."

❖   ❖   ❖

Abba Theodore of Pherme said that a man who is fulfilling a canon of penance is not chained by this canon; that is, one who repents sincerely, should he wish to undertake efforts greater than those assigned him, is not impeded by anything. And just as he should not think the canons to be but one, but as many as have been assigned to the Church by the Holy Spirit, so with the particular (canon) given to him.

❖   ❖   ❖

Two monks were beset by the demon of lust and, leaving the place of their ascetic struggles, went to the city and took women. After some time, they repented for this and said to one another: "What did we gain by abandoning the Angelic state and wallowing in the filth of sensual pleasures, which will occasion us, ultimately, to end up in the eternal fire and to suffer the unending tortures of Hell? Let us return once again to the desert and repent."

Indeed, they went to the desert, confessed their sins, and asked the Fathers to give them a canon of penance. The Elders ordered that these monks remain cloistered for an entire year in their cells and be given, as their food, only bread and water. (Coincidentally, the monks happened to resemble each other in the appearance of their faces.)

When the time assigned for their repentance had elapsed, they left their cells and the Fathers saw them. But curiously, though they resembled each other in their faces and had eaten the same food and had lived under the same conditions, nevertheless one of them looked pale, skeleton-like, and sickly, while the other one was robust and cheerful. The Fathers were amazed that, while they had eaten the same food and were both cloistered, they now differed so much in appearance.

They thus asked the skeleton-like monk: "What inner conversing did you have with your thoughts while you remained locked up in your cell for a year?"

He answered: "I thought continually about the sins which I had committed and about Hell, to which I am bound to go after death. From the fear of eternal punishment, my skin cleaved to my bones" [Psalm 101:5].

And they asked the other monk what he had thought about during one year of seclusion in his cell.

"I," he answered, "thanked God because He did not allow me to die in sin, but retrieved me from the filth of the world and from Hell and brought me once again to this Angelic state. And recalling without cessation the love of God, I rejoiced in spirit."

After these explanations, the Elders said: "The repentance of both of these two monks has equal merit before God."

❀   ❀   ❀

A brother fell to temptation; that is, to sin. So great was the sorrow that he suffered, that he abandoned his monastic rule. And though he wanted in principle to repent, he was impeded from so doing by his sorrow, saying within himself: "How can I restore myself to what I was before?" Being thus remiss and negligent, he did not have the power to take up his monastic work. So, he visited an Elder and confessed all that had befallen him.

The Elder, on listening to the matters which were tormenting the monk, related the following example to him in the form of an instructive parable: "A man," he began by saying, "had a field. On account of his neglect of it, it became fallow and was overrun by weeds and brambles. After some time, this man thought about attending to his field and cultivating it. So, he ordered his son to clean up the field. And, indeed, his son went to clean the field; but as soon as he saw that it was full of thorns, he was discouraged and said to himself: 'I would never be able to uproot all that and to clean this field.' So he lay down and went to sleep.

"After a bit, he awakened and, gazing again on the vast number of brambles, became depressed by it all and lay on the ground—sometimes sleeping and sometimes rolling over from one side to another, the way a door swings on its hinge, as in the proverb: 'As the door turneth upon its hinges, so doth the slothful upon his bed. The slothful hideth his hand in his bosom; it grieveth him to bring it again to his mouth' [Proverbs 26:14–16]. He spent several days thusly, without working and inactive.

"In the meantime, his father came along to check what he had done to the field. Finding his son idle and indecisive, he said to him: 'Why have you done nothing up to now, my child?'

"The son answered: 'Father, as soon as I started to work and saw this mass of wild weeds and brambles, I lost my desire to work, lay down, and fell asleep. And so right up to today I have still done nothing.'

"'Do not worry, my son,' the father replied, 'every day you can clear an area the width of your bed, and thus your work will progress without inactivity crushing you.' Indeed, the son followed his father's advice and in a short time had cleaned the field of brambles and weeds.

"And in this way, my brother, you can work little by little, without risking the danger of being negligent. And God, seeing your desire to work, will restore you to your former rank."

The monk carefully listened to these suggestions, persisted with patience, and applied the directions of the Elder. And indeed, by the Grace of God, he attained to the peace which he had sought.

# CHAPTER 4

## *LOVE*

Abba Agathon was asked how sincere love for one's neighbor might be made manifest, and this blessed man, who had attained to the queen of the virtues to a perfect degree, responded: "Love is to find a leper, to take his body, and gladly to give him your own."

✳ ✳ ✳

The following is related to us by Bishop Palladios of Helenopolis. Abba Serapion was an Egyptian ascetic of perfect accomplishment and great generosity. Many times he was seen wandering in a sheet wrapped around his naked body, because he had given his clothing away in an act of charity. For this reason he was also called "Sindonios" [from the Greek word for "sheet"].

✳ ✳ ✳

Palladios describes the reception of outsiders to the sketes and hermitages of Egypt and the Thebaid as follows: "When we reached Palestine from Egypt, we first visited Abba Apollo. As soon as they heard about our arrival, the monks from his *synodia* came out by rank to meet us. As they came near us, they bowed and greeted us. Again by rank, the oldest in front, the youngest in back, and we in the middle, they took us to the cells. The president of the assembly was waiting there for us. When he saw us, he made a profound prostration and kissed us. He took us to his cell and, as soon as he had offered the prayers appropriate to such an occasion, had us sit down. He then fetched water and washed our feet, after which he immediately led us to the refectory, where there awaited us, not a frugal meal, but well-prepared food.

"He showed similar hospitality to all of the monks and clergy who visited him. He constantly advised his monks: 'When monks come to visit, my children, make a prostration before them and show them veneration, as did the Patriarch Abraham to his visitors. Through them, you show veneration to God. If you have seen your brother, you have beheld also your God.'"

❁   ❁   ❁

"When you are visited by some brother, remove the sorrowful look from your face," one of the Elders advises, "and hide it in your heart until he leaves. Afterwards, return it to your face, since, when they see you with such a look, the demons fear to draw near you."

❀   ❀   ❀

Another Elder gives the following advice: "When you perceive that visitors are coming to visit you, before they knock on your door pray these words to God: 'O Lord, protect all of us from judgment and from evil tongues, that my brothers might depart this place in peace and gratified.'"

❁   ❁   ❁

Once the Fathers of the skete gave the order that the brothers were to observe a fast for one week, that is, to put nothing in their mouths—not even water. However, it so happened that during these days some monks from Egypt came to visit Abba Moses the Ethiopian. In order to feed them, the hospitable Abba prepared some lentils.

Upon seeing smoke coming from his hut, several not-so-virtuous brothers reported to the Elders: "Moses disobeyed your instructions and is preparing food."

On Sunday, when the whole skete gathered in the Church, the Priest, who knew the great virtue of the Saint, told him—when he approached to take *antidoron*—, loudly, so as to be heard by all: "Well done, Abba Moses, for you did not heed the command of man, but rather the commandment of God [that of love for others]."

❉   ❉   ❉

An inexperienced monk went to be counselled by Abba Poimen. It was around the middle of the Great Fast. Having confessed his thoughts and his soul having found rest, the young monk said to the Saint: "I nearly decided not to come here today, and I would have lost so much of a beneficial nature."

"Why, my child?" the Saint asked.

"The thought came to me that perhaps you would not receive me, Abba, since it is the Great Fast."

"We here, my child," Abba Poimen said, "are not accustomed to closing that little wooden door outside [that of hospitality], but this one...," putting his finger against his lips.

❊ ❊ ❊

Two strangers—monks—went to visit a certain Elder on a fasting day. He received them with eagerness and, abiding by the rules of hospitality, ate with them at the table. Afterwards, he explained to them that not only does fasting have its reward, but that one who relaxes the fast because of those whom he is entertaining receives a double reward. First, because he cuts off his own will, and second because, in giving rest to his brothers, he keeps the commandment of love.

❊ ❊ ❊

Two brothers of the skete asked the holy Macarios to sit at their table. He, so as not to disappoint them, nonetheless set the following condition for himself: for each glass of wine that they would give him to drink, to take no water into his mouth for an entire day. The brothers, who knew nothing of this, kept giving him wine, to please him. He drank it without concern for the fact that this would later bring torment upon him. His novice, however, on seeing his struggles, told the other monks: "For the love of Christ, brothers, do not give him wine to drink, for the next day he will begin to punish himself."

❊ ❊ ❊

Abba Silouan happened once to visit a cœnobitic monastery with his disciple, Zacharias. In the morning, when they were preparing to leave, the monks of the monastery insisted that they eat, even though it was a fasting day. The Saint and his disciple, in order not to insult the monks, accepted.

Later, as they were on their way, they saw a small spring. Zacharias, who was thirsty, asked permission from his Elder to drink some water.

"It is a fasting day today," the Saint reminded him.

"But a little while ago we ate, Abba."

"That was a meal of hospitality," the Saint explained. "Now, however, nothing prevents us from continuing our fast."

❖   ❖   ❖

A Bishop who was fond of those in the monastic life had the habit of visiting the sketes and monasteries in his eparchy once a year. During one such visit, exhausted by his long journey, he asked to rest for a short time in the cell of some hermit. The brother, having washed the Bishop's feet, set the table to entertain him hospitably. However, he had nothing to offer the Bishop, save the bread and salt that he was accustomed to eating himself.

"Your Grace, you will have to forgive me," the brother said, apologizing for his poor table.

Impressed by the great self-restraint of monastics, the Bishop told the brother: "May the time come when I will return and find not even salt."

❖   ❖   ❖

On a certain significant Feast Day, when the monks of the skete were sitting all together at a common table to eat, one brother said to the cook: "I never eat cooked food—only bread and salt."

So the cook called out loudly enough for his assistant to hear: "This brother doesn't eat cooked food. Bring the salt."

One of the great Elders then austerely said to the brother: "It would have been better for you to eat meat in your cell than to have made such a display in front of all of the brothers."

※　※　※

Another inexperienced monk, who had imposed on himself the discipline of not eating bread, went one day to visit a famous Elder. He found other visitors in the Elder's cell. The Elder cooked some food for his visitors. When they sat at the table, the inexperienced monk took out the soaked fava beans which he had brought with him and ate them. The Elder, who had been watching him, took the young man aside after the meal and advised him: "When you eat with other brothers, my child, avoid as much as possible showing your self-constraint, for vainglory lies in waiting to deprive you of your reward. If you are, however, resolved not to relax your ascetic disciplines, remain in your cell and avoid visiting others."

※　※　※

From the teachings of a wise Father: "When you find yourself among others, do not succumb to showing off your ascetic accomplishments. Do not, for example, let them know that you do not eat oil, or fish, or cooked food. Avoid drinking wine only, for the sake of the warfare of the flesh. If you should encounter some foolish person who condemns you for this, give no heed whatever to such condemnation."

※　※　※

"Never prefer gain for yourself over that which is beneficial for your brother," Saint Anthony the Great constantly used to say.

※　※　※

When Abba Theodore was still a novice, his Elder sent him to the skete bakery to bake his bread. He found someone else there who wanted to bake his own bread, but who could find no one to help him. The young Theodore put down his sack and gave the brother a hand. He had no sooner finished than another brother came. Theodore once again relinquished his turn and offered his help. One by one, there came a third brother, a fourth, and finally a sixth. Theodore helped all of the brothers and at last, after everyone else, baked his own bread. The sun had completely disappeared by the time he returned to his Elder. He explained to the Elder why he had been so long delayed, without even thinking that he had done anything of any worth.

＊　＊　＊

Many anecdotes are related about Abba Agathon and the great love which he harbored in his heart for his fellow man.

He once went down into the city to sell his baskets and happened upon an unfortunate man at the side of the road, ill and abandoned, whom, until that moment, not a single passer-by had deigned to help.

The holy man got him up, attended to him, and, with the money from his baskets, rented a room and took him in. It is said that he remained there for some time with the destitute man, caring for him, while at the same time working to meet their expenses. Later, when the stranger became wholly well and was in good enough condition to return to his own land, Abba Agathon then returned to his beloved silence.

＊　＊　＊

Yet another time, when the same Father went down to the city to sell some of his baskets and to procure a little bread, he found near the marketplace an old, poor cripple.

"For the love of God, Abba," the cripple began to plead on seeing the Saint, "don't you, too, leave this poor wretch unaided. Bring me near to you."

Abba Agathon picked the man up and sat him next to him in the place where he had set up his baskets to sell them.

"How much money did you make, Abba?" the cripple would ask each time that the Elder sold a basket.

"Such and such," the Elder would tell him.

"That's good enough," the cripple finally said. "Won't you buy me a little pie, Abba? That would be good of you, since I have not eaten since last evening."

"With pleasure," the Saint told him, immediately fulfilling the cripple's request.

Shortly thereafter, the cripple requested some fruit. And then something sweet. Thus, for each basket that was sold, the Saint spent the proceeds, until, thanks to his patronage, all of the baskets and the money were gone, without his having kept even two pennies for himself. More importantly, he did this all with great eagerness, even though he knew that he would thus go perhaps two weeks without any bread for himself.

Since he had sold his last basket, the Saint got ready to leave the marketplace.

"So you're going?" the cripple asked him.

"Yes, I have completed all of my work."

"Uh, do me the favor of taking me as far as the crossroads, and you can leave for the desert from there," the strange old man again pleadingly said.

The good Agathon took the cripple on his back and carried him to the place where he wanted to go, though with great difficulty, since he was exhausted from his day's work.

As soon as he reached the crossroads and started to put down his living burden, he heard a sweet voice say to him:

"May you be blessed, Agathon, by God, both on earth and in Heaven."

The Saint raised up his eyes to see who it was who had spoken with him. The would-be old man had completely disappeared, since he was an Angel sent by God to test the Saint's love.

❀    ❀    ❀

It was said by someone that Abba Agathon lived and acted only to please his neighbor. When he occasioned to be crossing the river with other brothers, he was the first to take in his hands the boat's oars. When visitors would go to his cell, he greeted them with one hand while with the other he set a table for them, so as to show them hospitality.

Once he was given a hoe to help him tend his garden.

"What a nice hoe," a brother who happened to see it in his hands one day told the Saint.

Abba Agathon would not under any circumstances permit him to leave, if he did not take with him the hoe which he had so much liked.

❀   ❀   ❀

Abba Apollo, too, they say, had such love for his fellow man that he never in his life refused help to anyone, whether the service to be rendered was small or large.

When the brothers asked for his aid, he offered it immediately, always saying with a smile: "Together with my Lord, I shall work today for the benefit of my soul."

❀   ❀   ❀

"Why, Abba, do monks of our day, though they labor, not receive from God the spiritual gifts received by the Fathers of old?" a brother asked an Elder.

"In the old days, my child," the pious Elder replied, "there was love between monks, and each one was eager to help his brother to ascend to higher things. Today, love has grown cold and one monk lures another into lowly things, and for this reason God no longer grants spiritual gifts."

✳   ✳   ✳

"In the old days," Abba John said to a young monk who had gone to him for counsel, "spiritual business was the primary work of the monk, while physical labor was an avocation. Today these priorities have been reversed, and the work of the soul is considered an avocation, while handiwork has become an occupation."

"What is it that is the work of the soul?" the brother asked.

"That which is done according to the Divine command," the Elder explained.

"Let us say, for example, that you learn that I am ill and your conscience tells you that you should visit me. You, however, sit and muse: 'If I go, I will get behind in my work, since I will lose time.' You do not come and you violate the commandment of love. Or, say, someone asks you to help him with his work. You say to yourself: 'Now, must I leave in the middle of my work to go help someone else?' You overlook the command of God, which is the work of the soul, and concentrate on your handiwork, which is of secondary importance."

※   ※   ※

Saint Macarios once went to keep an ailing Elder company. Casting a glance about the Elder's cell, the Saint saw that there was nothing, not even a trace of food.

"What would you like to eat, brother?" Macarios asked.

The ill man hesitated to answer. After all, what could he ask for, since there was nothing in his hermitage? Finally, because the Saint persisted in asking, he mentioned that he would like some flour soup. But where was flour to be found?

Saint Macarios, to comfort his sick brother, went to Alexandria, going fifty miles by foot to find flour.

※   ※   ※

Saint Poimen lived in asceticism with his four brothers in the Egyptian desert. Paisios, the youngest brother, had not yet corrected many of his shortcomings and upset the others with his unruly behaviors.

"This young man doesn't leave us any peace," Abba Poimen said with agitation to his older brother one day.

"Come, and we will leave this place, so that our minds can find some peace."

They took to the road and attempted to find a place that would be appropriate to settle. Paisios, however, caught on that his brothers had abandoned him and had left, and set out to search for them.

Abba Poimen saw him coming from afar and said to Abba Anoub, the older brother: "Let's wait for our brother, who is trying to reach us."

Finally the young brother reached them and complained: "Where are you going, and why did you leave me alone?"

"We are leaving, so that we can find some peace. You constantly bother us with your rash behaviors," Abba Poimen told him.

"Yes, yes. All of you go where you wish," the young man said guilelessly.

Seeing the brother's innocence, Abba Poimen said to his older brother: "Let us return, Anoub. I think that this youth misbehaves unintentionally, or that God allows his behaviors so as to see our patience."

So, they returned to their cell and all of them lived together to their last.

❋   ❋   ❋

The disciple of a certain Elder lived in a hut some ten miles distant from the skete. One day his Elder decided to send for him to come and to fetch some bread. However, the Elder reflected some: "For a little bread, should I make the brother walk ten miles? Leave him be. I will go for it myself." He threw his knapsack over his shoulder and started out. On his way, he stumbled on a rock and opened such a wound on his foot that it was impossible to stop the bleeding. From the intense pain that he felt, he began to cry.

"Why are you crying, Abba?" he heard a sweet voice ask from behind him.

He turned his head and saw a beautiful Angel. However, he was not frightened, and he pointed to the wound with his finger.

"Stop crying about that insignificant thing," the Angel commanded him. "The steps that you have taken out of love for your brother I have counted, and you will receive your reward from God."

The Elder took courage and joyfully continued on his way. From then on he was always eager to serve the brothers.

One day he once again got bread and set out to take some to another hermit who lived a very long distance away. It happened that he, too, was coming to the Elder with the same intention in mind. The two encountered one another on the road.

"My brother," the Elder said first, "with labor I tried to build up a little treasure and you managed to take it from me."

"Does the narrow way perhaps have room only for you, Abba? Make a little room for us to pass through, too," the brother replied.

While they were saying this an Angel again came, saying to them: "Disputes like this one are like sweet-smelling incense rising up to Heaven."

❈    ❈    ❈

When Saint Sabbas the Sanctified was a novice in the Monastery of Saint Euthymios, still very young in age, he was assigned to prepare bread for the brothers. One rainy day, while he was kneading bread, a brother went into the bakery and put his wet clothes on the oven to dry. Sabbas, who had not seen what this brother had done, lighted the oven. In the meantime, the brother came to get his clothes and, on seeing the oven lighted, almost cried, since he had no other clothes and those which he was wearing were borrowed.

Seeing the worry of the brother, Saint Sabbas lost no time. With a bound he reached into the oven and pulled out the clothes.

And what a miracle! Neither had the clothes been damaged by the fire, nor did the most sympathetic young novice suffer anything. The flames did not burn him—not so much because of his piety, as with the Three Children of old, but because of his love for his brother.

❈    ❈    ❈

Three brothers agreed to clear fifteen acres of land. The first day that they undertook the work, however, one of the three happened to fall ill and was obliged to return to the skete.

The two who remained said between themselves: "Can we not make a little extra effort to clear that part of the land assigned to our brother? With his blessing, we will complete that portion."

They informed him and did so. When they finished clearing the land, they summoned their brother to receive his pay.

"What pay?" he asked. "After all, I did not take part in the clearing."

"With your blessing, the work was properly done," the two others answered. "Come on, now, and get your pay."

Since the brother would not agree to take the pay, and since the other two brothers insisted on giving it to him, in order not to quarrel they went to a neighboring Elder, to ask him to settle the dispute.

"Abba," the brother who had fallen ill began, "the three of us went to clear some land. But I, before even taking a sickle into my hand, became ill and left. The brothers here are now trying to force me to take part of the pay, even though I did no work. Do you find this right?"

"Abba," the others continued, "the three of us together contracted to clear fifteen acres. Had we all worked together, it is indeed doubtful that we could have finished in the prescribed amount of time. But, with the blessing of the brother, we brought it to completion much more quickly. Is it not right, then, that he should have his pay?"

The Elder marvelled at the love of these brothers. He immediately took the wooden mallet [used in Orthodox monasteries to strike a long piece of wood to call the monastics to gatherings and services] and signalled for the brethren to gather in assembly.

"Come, Fathers and brothers, we are having a trial today," he told them when they had gathered, and he explained to them the problem.

The result was that the brother was forced to take his pay. He took it weeping, continuously saying that the brothers had on that day done him an injustice.

❀   ❀   ❀

Four friends once decided to undertake the ascetic life. Three of them entered into the hermitic life, while the fourth one took it upon himself to serve them. He would take their handiwork to the marketplace of the neighboring village and then deliver all necessary provisions to the hermitage.

After a few years, two of the four died, leaving only the friend who had placed himself in the others' service and one of the hesychasts. The caretaker, who was the youngest of all, once fell to a great sin in the village where he would go to sell the handiwork.

A holy hermit, who had received from God the gift of visions, so that he saw with the eyes of his soul that which one cannot see with bodily eyes, had also situated his hut near the hermitage. To this holy man it was revealed that the two hesychasts in Heaven had entreated God to allow the brother who had fallen to be devoured by a wild beast, so that his sin would be cleansed by his blood and he would not lose Paradise and be separated from them.

So, as the caretaker was returning from the village, he was confronted suddenly by a beastly lion, which was ready to tear him to pieces. However, the other brother, who was waiting for him above at the hermitage, saw from afar the danger and, stricken with terror, fell on the floor and prayed for God to deliver his brother from the teeth of the beast.

The clairvoyant Elder was all of this time beholding the two brothers in Heaven, saying fervently: "Lord, have mercy and allow him to be torn to pieces by the beast, so that his sin can be atoned for."

"Lord, save your servant from the teeth of the beast," the hesychast below cried out, perspiring in agony.

Then something unforeseen took place. Though the fearful African lion had almost pinned down his victim by the neck with his front legs, he suddenly turned about and disappeared into the nearby jungle, as though some invincible force had driven him away.

And the holy hermit heard a voice say to the two brothers in Heaven: "It is right that the petition of one who still struggles below on the earth in the flesh be granted. For you, the repose and blessedness of this place suffice."

Filled with contrition and repentance for his fall, and, of course, after the danger which he had beheld with his own eyes, the caretaker returned to his brother and, having confessed his sin to his brother, locked himself in his cell and wept for his sin until the end of his life.

After a few years the two friends who had survived also died, and the holy hermit saw the four of them together in Heaven.

❧     ❧     ❧

Two young monks went down to the city to sell their baskets. They separated for a while, and during this period one of them fell to a serious sin of the flesh. Afterwards, darkened by despair, he wished under no circumstances to return to the desert.

"Go back alone. I will remain here," he told the other monk as soon as they met again.

"Why, my brother? What happened to you?" the other monk asked him kindly, without having an inkling as to the reason for his fellow monk's decision not to return to the desert.

"Ah, since you insist on knowing, when we separated I went to a woman. Now I have just lost my soul. What is there for me in the desert?"

The pure monk was shaken on hearing of the sin to which his friend had fallen. However, he did not show this. Indeed, to save his friend from the rapacious clutches of despair, he pretended that the same thing had also happened to him.

"Let us return to the desert, brother," he said with tears in his eyes, "and let us both struggle together. God, a Father who loves men, will see our repentance and will forgive us."

With these and other words of comfort, he convinced the truly guilty monk to follow him to the desert. When they reached the skete, they both confessed and were put under a severe penance by the Fathers.

For an entire year the innocent monk repented and struggled for the sake of his guilty brother, taking upon himself all of the shame for a sin that he had not even contemplated. God accepted his offering and rewarded the monk in the following way:

One night, as one of the great Fathers of the skete there prayed, he heard a voice tell him, "Because of the great love of the innocent monk, I forgive the guilty one."

After this, the Fathers granted a release from their penance to the two monks, never learning which one was indeed the guilty person.

❀　❀　❀

"I have never lain down to sleep having some feeling of grief in my heart about my neighbor," Abba Agathon said. "And, by the same token, to the extent that I could control such, I have never let another person fall asleep upset with me."

❀　❀　❀

Abba Isaac also always said: "I have never let a thought enter here into this cell against a brother who might have upset me. At the same time, I have been careful to see that a brother never goes to his cell with a bad thought about me.

❀　❀　❀

Abba John went along with several brothers to visit a certain far-off skete. While they were walking, it got dark, and the monk who was leading them got lost. The brothers understood that he was lost and pointedly asked of the Elder: "What should we do now, Abba? If we continue to follow him, we will run the risk of being lost in this vast desert."

"If we let on that we know he has lost his way, the brother will be embarrassed and become upset," the good Elder said. "Better, I will pretend that I am tired and cannot walk any farther, and propose that we stay here until the sun comes up."

And this is what they did, so as not to upset their inattentive guide.

❀    ❀    ❀

Before Abba Poimen and his four brothers established their skete, a certain anchorite had lived there. He was a good confessor and many of the Christians from the surrounding cities would go to him to confess and to take counsel with him. From the time that Saint Paisios went to the skete, however, the people had abandoned the anchorite and went to the Saint. This troubled the Saint, who often told the brothers: "What are we to do about this great Elder? The people have put me in a bad position. We must do something to make up for all of this to the Elder."

One day, they prepared a well-cooked meal, put a little wine in a carafe, and went all together to visit the neighboring anchorite. When he saw them coming in the distance, however, the anchorite hid and told his disciple to tell them that he was not free to receive visitors.

"Brother, tell your Elder," Saint Poimen told the disciple, "that we are content to wait for him out here all day. We will not return to our cells, until we have been found worthy to take his blessing."

The anchorite, seeing their love and humility, came out and received them with joy. The visitors prostrated before him and entreated him to deign to eat with them from the food that they had brought. Moved by the kindness of the brothers, the anchorite offered, instead of the usual toast, the following words at the meal: "It behooves me to confess that not only is all that I have heard about you true, but also many other things which I have verified with my own eyes. You are truly men of God, not only in theory, but in practice."

From that time, the anchorite and Saint Poimen were the closest of friends.

❀   ❀   ❀

Twelve monks were crossing an unfamiliar desert for the first time. When it got dark, their guide became confused and took an opposite road. The brothers quickly understood this, but each separately tried the whole night to hide it, so as not to embarrass the guide. When the sun came up the guide's error became obvious.

"Forgive me, brothers," the guide told them with embarrassment. "It seems that I took the opposite road."

"We know," they replied, "but do not worry. We will simply turn around."

And without having shown even the slightest displeasure that they had wandered aimlessly the whole night, the brothers set out on a new route.

The guide, amazed at their politeness, said over and over: "Men of God will control themselves even to the point of death in order not to upset their brother."

❀   ❀   ❀

A hermit one day sent his novice down to the city to bring back a camel to the skete, so that they could take their baskets to the market.

Returning, the novice encountered another hermit, a neighbor of theirs, who said to him: "It is a shame that you did not let me know that you were going down to the city. I would have asked you to bring back a camel for me, too, so that I could take my baskets to the market."

The novice related this to his Elder. The Elder ordered the novice immediately to give the camel to their neighbor, and to tell him that their own load of baskets was taken care of.

"Go with him to the city, and as soon as he is finished, bring the animal back so that we can transport our goods, too."

The novice eagerly fulfilled the command of his Elder. When the neighbor had finished his work, the novice took the camel back.

"Where are you going, brother?" the neighbor asked.

"Back to the skete to transport our baskets, with your blessing, Abba," said the youth, leaving hurriedly to get everything done.

As soon as the neighbor heard that the novice and Elder had abandoned their work in mid-course to help him, he was troubled. When he returned to the desert, he went to the Elder and, making a prostration, told him: "Forgive me, brother, but your great love earned the fruit of my labors."

❀   ❀   ❀

A brother, just as he was preparing to sew the handles on the straw baskets that he was making ready for the market, heard his neighbor say to himself: "Lazy me! Here the market is under way and I have not prepared handles for my baskets."

So, the brother took his own handles and went to his neighbor.

"I have these left over," he told his neighbor. "Do you perhaps need them?"

The neighbor accepted these with relief, as a gift sent from God, without suspecting that his brother had left his own work unfinished in order to comfort him.

❀   ❀   ❀

Two fellow ascetics were once working all night on their handiwork. They were spinning strands from hemp, so that they could later weave these into ropes. But the strands of one of the brothers kept breaking continually. He began to lose patience and to get angry at his brother, whose work was progressing normally. The other brother saw this and, in order not to be a source of upset for the impatient brother, similarly broke off his own strands of hemp each time that his brother broke his. Thus their work went forward at an equal pace and the two finished their work without anything unpleasant occurring between them.

❋   ❋   ❋

An inexperienced monk once went to a certain Elder to get direction. They spoke with one another for many hours about many things regarding their lives. Benefited and with contentment of soul, the young monk got up to leave.

"Forgive me, Abba," he said as he made a prostration to the Elder. "I took you from your prayer with my visit today."

"My prayer, child," the good Elder replied with kindness, "is to give you comfort and to send you back to your cell benefited in soul."

❖   ❖   ❖

Saint Abramios left the world at a very young age and became a dweller in the desert. There, with his ascetic labors and with the aid of Grace, he attained to a great measure of virtue.

After many years of having heard no news about his relatives, he learned that his only brother had died and left his young daughter, not more than six or seven years old, in the streets. A friend of the Saint rescued the orphan and one day took her to the desert.

The hermit, in spite of the hard life that he had led, had a very tender heart. He felt sorry for the motherless little child, who had found no merciful soul to look after her, so he kept her with him, disregarding all of the difficulties which he had to face in rearing her in such a desolate place. Having thus made a decision to adopt the girl, the Elder became for her sake a tender mother, a loving father, a good educator, and a wise teacher. He built a suitable little house for her next to his desert cell. He was careful to see that she lacked nothing from those things needed in the rearing of a young child, neither healthy food nor appropriate clothing. He taught her to read and write and brought her up in a Christian way, cultivating her unformed soul with daily teaching. He came to love her greatly and he wanted to make her an exemplar of virtue and piety, one day to see her a true ascetic, a second Saint Sarah, who was at the time renowned throughout Egypt for her wisdom and for the holiness of her life.

Time passed quickly and Maria—this is what the orphaned child's name was—grew up. It seemed that she would become, as her good uncle, at least, had expected, a prudent young woman.

But the Devil resented the philanthropic work of the Saint and brought his strongest powers forth to make the girl his own, thus to embitter the Elder and cause him to regret his kindness and to lose his reward for it.

A young hypocrite began to visit the Saint's hermitage, supposedly to take advantage of his wise counsel. In actuality, however, he was frequenting the place because he had once seen the beautiful girl and was sure that, guileless as she seemed to be, it would require little to take her in. And it did not take long for evil to manifest itself.

With no reason for concern, the Elder went deep into the desert for a few days. It was an old custom of his. There he engaged in his spiritual exercises: prayer and the lifting up of his soul. In the meantime, Maria remained completely alone. Satan's tool—the young man—, for his part, lost no time. Finding an opportune moment and the right bait, as did the serpent with Eve, he seduced her. Afterwards, as is always the case, the guilty young man managed to disappear. The young girl then came to her senses and realized that she had wallowed in the mud. But it was too late. Reflecting on the sin to which she had fallen, she shuddered. And instead of repenting and seeking refuge in Divine mercy, the unfortunate girl threw herself wholly into the arms of black despair. She saw the holiness all about her mercilessly condemning her, the desert reproaching her, and heard Satan whispering in her troubled mind: "There is no salvation for you any longer. You are wholly lost."

Oh, if only she could have escaped hearing that voice repeating continually, in a monotone, maliciously, and without sympathy: "You are wholly lost."

The tragic girl decided to seek refuge by fleeing. She departed in the middle of the dark night, without leaving a trace of any kind.

During this time, the Saint had separated himself from every earthly thought. His spirit had ascended into the immaterial world. His soul was to be found in ceaseless ecstasy.

The third day, the Saint began to feel a sense of fatigue in his body and spirit. He abandoned his prayer for awhile, sat down on a large rock, rested his head on his knees, and fell asleep. He had no idea how many hours went by. Suddenly he stood up, terrified. A strange dream had unsettled him. He dreamed that he was in Maria's little garden and that he was waiting under the almond tree to read to her, as he did when she was young. Some distance above, a pure white dove was skipping about on top of the fence, unconcerned with anything. It seemed to be proud of its pure whiteness, which sparkled in the bright rays of the afternoon sun. But suddenly, there where no one would expect such a thing, a large snake slithered out of its hole. With an adroit strike, the snake caught the unsuspecting bird in its huge mouth, swallowed it whole in one gulp, and disappeared again into its nest.

"Oh my!" the tender-hearted Elder said.

And picking up his staff, he poked into the snake's hole. It, then, as though forced by some mysterious power, slithered out again and vomited forth the dove, alive, from its entrails. The dove was intact and as white as before, though its beautiful feathers were a bit ruffled.

Recovering from the dream, the Saint felt an uneasiness in his soul. Without any reason, his thoughts turned to Maria. "Something bad has happened to her," he said to himself worriedly.

Without losing time, he took his staff in hand and headed for home. As soon as he arrived, he went directly to Maria's house and knocked. Inside the little house complete silence reigned. He called out to the young girl by name many times. No answer. Uneasy, he opened the door and went inside. The house was deserted. He went to the garden and searched everywhere that he was used to finding her. Nothing. Everywhere quietness. Complete silence.

The Elder spent the night in agony. The next day he waited with certainty for her return. The same thing the next day. But she never appeared. Now there was no doubt that Maria had left. The young girl whom he had reared with such affection had fallen into the net of the wily dragon. The snake and the dove would not leave the pained Elder's mind.

The Elder was beyond consolation. For two whole years the tears did not dry in his eyes. His tender heart was torn to pieces when he would bring to mind the dangers to the soul and body to which the unprotected young girl was subject. He sent his acquaintances all over looking for her. He himself remained locked within his cell and found relief only in prayer. He tripled his ascetic labors. He exhausted his old man's body, that Christ might take mercy on him and return to the fold the poor lost sheep.

After several more years, a friend from among those who knew of his pain and who had been looking for the girl appeared at the Elder's cell. The news which he brought was such that the Elder's displeasure cannot be imagined. Maria was in Aiso—a very distant city—, living in a house of ill-repute. In other words, she had become a streetwalker.

A two-edged knife plunged into the Elder's heart would not have cut it into so many pieces as this information. He tried, however, to find courage in himself, so as not to be completely overcome by all of this.

"So be it," he sighed. "At least she is found."

He then made a momentous decision: That he would go to extract her from the mire, even if he had to go into the mud himself and breathe in all of its stench. He had to save her and to take her back to the harbor of peace, to the hallowed desert.

"O my Christ, Thou Who didst descend to the earth for the sake of the debauched, help me in my difficult journey," he prayed with his soul.

Without losing time on plans and tactics, he borrowed a few coins and an old soldier's uniform from his friend, rented a fast horse, and headed down to the city. This man, who for fifty whole years had not gone beyond the door of his cell, save to withdraw to the deepest desert, was now wandering among the streets of an unfamiliar city and asking passers-by—indeed, how great is the power of love!—where he could find the local house of ill-repute.

When he found it, he assumed the appearance of a lustful old man, went directly to the pander, gave him the appropriate funds, and ordered a rich dinner and the beautiful girl. The pimp surveyed the old man from head to toe with obvious disgust.

"Isn't he at least embarrassed by his gray hair?" he murmured.

However, not to lose his customer, the pimp was ready to accommodate him. The Saint saw all of the disdain in the visage of this perverted fellow, and his soul wept.

"O my Christ," he prayed secretly, "look upon my humility and grant success to my difficult mission."

So as to kindle no suspicion, the Elder sat and ate the meat and the other food which they had given him and drank all of the wine. And just think about the fact that he had for so many years sustained himself in the desert with dry bread and salt and had drunk water only with moderation. Anyway, he was then led to the chamber of sins. There the former orphan received him with all of the shamelessness of women of her occupation and with a good dose of mockery. His completely gray hair and beard struck her. And he, seeing her in such a pitiful condition, struggled to keep back his tears, so that they would not flow forth at such an inopportune time. The sinful woman took this all as shyness, and to encourage him she went over to embrace him. Then she stopped, thunderstruck by astonishment. There came forth from the Saint the pure fragrance of the desert, which was so well known to her. The fragrance at that moment covered all of the stench of the aromas of her trade.

The Saint immediately understood what was happening within her and abandoned his pretense, addressing her with great pain in his soul: "Maria, my child, do you not know me? For your sake I abandoned the desert, my silence, and came here to this place of sin to show you the road of repentance and return. Have mercy on this old man and do not make the last years of my life bitter. Do not overlook the labor and the shame which I have endured on your behalf."

The wanton girl would have wished the earth to open up and swallow her rather than to stand opposite this man, who had taught her purity and modesty. Out of her shame, she dared not even lift her eyes to look at him or to utter a word. She remained motionless and speechless for a long time: a virtual statue of stupefaction and pain. When she recovered from the initial shock, she fell at the feet of the Holy Elder and, like the prostitute in the Gospel, flooded them with her tears. Her heart became contrite. O how she wished to be delivered!

"There is salvation for all. No sin, no fall can surpass the power of the sacrifice of Him Who took upon His shoulders human wretchedness, that He might expiate it," the Elder said. He had so much more to tell her, but they had no time to lose. Before being discovered by the proprietors of the house, they slipped out through a small door known to Maria, and took the return road to the desert.

The girl's repentance was sincere. With the Grace of God and the guidance of the Elder, not only did she regain her former measure of virtue, but in many ways surpassed it. Thus there were realized in her the words of the Apostle, so comforting to all: "...but where sin abounded, Grace did much more abound" [Romans 5:20].

Saint Abramios passed the last years of his life in peace and grateful for the progress of his spiritual child.

❁    ❁    ❁

A very simple and guileless monk continually went to Abba John the Short to gain benefits from the Abba's wise counsel. The Abba always received him with affection and never ceased teaching him. Every time the monk went, there was something new for him to hear about the spiritual life. But the monk understood very little of all that the Elder had to say, and most of that he would forget. Thus he always asked about the same things over and over.

Once the monk stopped his visits. The Elder was surprised by this. So, one Sunday, encountering the monk in Church, he asked: "It is a long time since I have seen you, brother. What happened to you? Perhaps you have been ill?"

"No, Abba," the monk answered with hesitation, "but as you see, my head is thick and does not easily grasp your counsel. I am embarrassed to return continually to ask you about the same things."

"Take this," Abba John told him, pointing to a lamp that was in one corner of the Church, "and light it."

"Go now and bring the lamps of all the brothers and light them from this one here." The guileless monk immediately fulfilled the command of the Elder.

"Could it be that the light of this one lamp is now diminished, after having lighted so many others from it?" the Elder asked.

"Certainly not," the brother said, smiling.

"Nor does John lose anything, even if he gives advice over and over to the entire skete. So, you come along without any hesitation."

After that, the brother went regularly to the Elder and, with his help, became an excellent monk.

❧　❧　❧

"I do not fear God," the great teacher of the desert, Saint Anthony the Great, would tell his disciples, "because I love Him. Perfect love 'casteth out fear'" [1 St. John 4:18].

❧　❧　❧

Saint Ammoun of Nitria once went to visit Saint Anthony the Great and, since they enjoyed the intimacy of friendship, dared to ask him: "How is it that, though I put forth more effort than you, people think more of you than I?"

"It seems that I must love God more than you do," this friend of God answered with a kind smile.

❧　❧　❧

An elderly hermit once asked in his prayer for God to show him all of the ancient Fathers of the desert. He was then shown all of them, except for Saint Anthony the Great.

"Wait! Where is Saint Anthony?" he questioned with astonishment.

"Where God is," he heard a voice assuring him.

❀   ❀   ❀

"Love of God," Saint Maximos the Confessor writes, "is a virtuous tendency of the soul, and he who has it desires nothing of
created things over the love of God. However, it is impossible to
maintain such love when one feels even the slightest inclination
toward worldly things. He who loves God lives an Angelic life on
earth. He fasts, is watchful, prays, and always has good thoughts
about his fellow man."

ﾉ*

PARADISE CAMP FIRE    2018

STAR SURVIVOR
JACKPACK ♡
TURTLE

plastron

côté

STAR
SURVIVORS

ampre